INDIAN JEWS:
AN ANNOTATED BIBLIOGRAPHY
1665-2005

Indian Jews:
An Annotated Bibliography
1665-2005

NATHAN KATZ

MANOHAR
2013

Publication of this work has been supported by the Foundation for Remote Jewish Communities and the Society for Indo-Judaic Studies

First published 2013

ISBN 978-81-7304-980-4

Published by
Ajay Kumar Jain *for*
Manohar Publishers & Distributors
4753/23 Ansari Road, Daryaganj
New Delhi 110 002

Typeset by
Ajay Arts
New Delhi-110002

Printed by
Salasar Imaging Systems
Delhi-110035

Contents

Acknowledgements

The Foundation for Remote Jewish Communities very kindly and generously provided a grant to subvent publication costs. My deepest gratitude to its directors, Rabbi Marvin Tokayer and Michael Kong.

This is the third book of mine in the field of Indo-Judaic Studies that Manohar Publishers of New Delhi is bringing out. I salute them for their vision and professionalism.

Over the years, several people have sent me copies of articles, and even at the risk of overlooking someone, my thanks go to: Rabbi Marvin Tokayer, Samuel M. Daniel, and Ranjith Henry. The original idea was for this to be a full collaboration with Frank Joseph Shulman, but circumstances intervened. Nevertheless, his contribution to this work is significant. Arlene Belzer is an insightful and diligent editor, and I thank her for her unflappable professionalism.

NATHAN KATZ

Introduction

INDIAN JEWS IN WESTERN WRITINGS

The 'modern' Western world was introduced to Indian Jews in 1665 when Menasseh ben Israel of Amsterdam petitioned Oliver Cromwell's government to permit Jews to return to England from where they had been expelled in 1290, citing the tolerant Maharajas of Cochin as an example to be emulated. In 1687, Moses Perreyra de Paiva published a Portuguese-language account of a visit to Cochin by a group of reconversos from Amsterdam the year before. Not long after, in 1738, a Danish missionary named J.A. Sarortius wrote in English about a community he called 'B'nai Israel' in western India, which may or may not have been the 'lost' Jewish community of the Konkan coast known today by the Anglicized term 'Bene Israel'. Then in 1768, the leader of the Cochin community, Ezekiel Rahabi, wrote a Hebrew letter to a co-religionist with whom he had commercial links in Holland, and his letter was soon published in Germany.

While there had been ongoing contact between India's Jews and their Middle Eastern and European counterparts throughout the ages, it was only when accounts of them appeared in European books and newspapers that they slowly emerged into the often myopic awareness of the 'modern' world. Even so, Indian Jews were generally regarded simply as an exotic curiosity until recently. Now we know them as another Diasporic community with its own history, traditions, folkways and literature, but very much a part of the Jewish world.

Works by Indian Jews themselves, such as Haeem Kehimkar and Benjamin J. Israel, were not widely known. Then, based on the pioneering academic work by Walter J. Fischel and Solomon D. Goitein, and by the 1980s new scholarship by Barbara C. Johnson, Shalva Weil, Joan G. Roland, Nathan Katz and Ellen S. Goldberg, and others, made the academic world aware of their contributions, culture, and history. Since then, their experience has been explored in novels, memoirs and films, as well as in scholarship.

During the 1990s, 'lost tribes' were 'discovered' in Mizoram and Andhra Pradesh and many of them immigrated to Israel into a politically and messianically-charged context, resulting in a plethora of Judaizing movements worldwide. There was a rapprochement in diplomacy between India and Israel, and countless post-military Israeli youth made journeys to India, and Israelis of Indian origin became commercial, agricultural and cultural bridges between their two homelands. The world witnessed a tragic terrorist attack on Mumbai, including the Chabad House, in 2008. Increasingly, Western Jewish tourists paid their respects at synagogues in India. With these currents of the past twenty years, India's Jewish communities are no longer obscure to the Western imagination. Just as the Indo-Israeli relationship has moved from the margins to the forefront, so Indian Jews have developed links with co-religionists around the globe.

ABOUT THIS BIBLIOGRAPHY

This bibliography is designed to assist students and scholars who wish to explore India's rich and varied Jewish heritage. It is also intended for the more casual reader, especially Indian Jews themselves whether at home in India or relocated in Israel, the United States, England or Australia. It begins with Menasseh ben Israel's 1665 book, and 2005 was selected as a point of closure. During the early twenty-first century, the study of Indian Jewish communities has become mainstream as scholars of religions have become fascinated by the persistence and cultural adaptations of India's tiniest community and as Jewish studies scholars have sought more inclusive paradigms for understanding the Jewish Diaspora. A similar surge of interest among scholars of South Asia is just beginning, but knowledge about Judaism and Indian Jewish communities remains undeveloped, although Indian scholars have begun to contribute in significant ways to Indo-Judaic Studies.

Many of the items in this bibliography are difficult to obtain, some impossible. For example, even New York University owns no copy of one of its own Masters' thesis about Indian Jews (Neumann 1960). Newspaper articles are often obscure and even harder to locate, and no exhaustive list is possible. Often as not, a photocopy of a photocopy is privately circulated, but lacking publication data. Some of the works mentioned below are manuscripts found in Indian synagogues and homes, some are very old, valuable books that do not circulate from libraries. Fortunately, scholarly studies are generally accessible.

Beyond the problem of accessibility, one is easily daunted by the number of languages in which these works were written. English, of course, is the predominant language of modern scholarship as well as the *lingua franca* among educated Indians, Jews included. One also finds many sources in Hebrew, be they indigenous writings or Israeli scholarship. Then again, there are sources in French, German, Portuguese, Dutch, Yiddish, Persian, Arabic, Marathi and Malayalam. This bibliography excludes liturgical works and synagogal records; these works for the most part are found in research libraries such as the Ben-Zvi Institute in Jerusalem, or in private collections or antiquarian catalogues.

This bibliography is organized by communities. First are general works on Indian Jewry, followed by sections on the Cochin Jews, the Bene Israel, the little-known Mughal Jews, the Baghdadi communities of Indian port cities, the Ashkenazim, many of whom—but not all—were refugees to India from Nazi-dominated Europe, and finally recent Judaizing movements of north-east India and in Andhra Pradesh.

Excluded from this bibliography are documents pertaining to Indo-Israeli diplomacy, except in so far as it bears on the religious and cultural life of Indian Jews, as well as comparisons of Judaism with Indian religions. Also excluded are liturgical works, synagogue record books and archived government records, and manuscripts. Fascinating comparative studies of Judaism with Hinduism/ Jainism/Buddhism likewise await cataloguing, as do the few experiments with comparative literature from these two highly literate and prolific cultures. We also see scholarship on interreligious dialogues among Jews, Hindus, Jains, and Buddhists emerging during recent years. All of these comprise the field of 'Indo-Judaic Studies', but this bibliography focuses on Jewish communities in India.

Each section, as appropriate, is subdivided as follows:

- First are listed sources of incidental bearing on Indian Jewry—for example, a work on Indian history which makes mention of them, or a study of Jewish commerce of the middle ages which mentions the India trade, etc.
- Second are memoirs by Indian Jews and accounts by Jewish travellers from years past, many of which make for charming reading.
- Third are works of modern scholarship, followed by the fourth category, auto-historical works. Fifth, there are general interest works: magazine and newspaper articles and popular works. There is a good deal of overlap between the third and fourth categories, and the reader is advised that in assigning a category, no judgement is implied as to the value of a given work. Indeed, works such as Kehimkar's or Koder's contain valuable data and insights. The difference between a scholarly and a general interest

piece is essentially stylistic, and for the most part the writings of Indian Jews (e.g., S.S. Koder, N.E. Roby, A.I. Simon, H.S. Kehimkar, B.J. Israel, S. Samuel, A.S. Abraham) have been assigned to the latter classification—although a few (F. Hallegua, E.D. Ezra, E.N. Musleah) could be considered 'scholarly'. Some could just as easily be considered 'primary documents', since they present their community's historical self-understanding uncritically or defensively.

- Finally, documentary films are listed.

Despite its obvious shortcomings and incompleteness, I am pleased to make available the fruits of several decades of work. Colleagues in the small field of Indian-Jewish studies may find their work lightened a bit by this bibliography. At the same time, Indian Jews themselves are avid historians and enjoy reading about themselves—as we all do—and this bibliography is also for them. Finally, the general reader will learn more than they imagined possible about *Galut Hodu*, the remarkable Jewish experience in India.

CHAPTER 1

Indian Jewry in General

SOURCES WITH INCIDENTAL REFERENCE TO INDIAN JEWRY

One is struck by the variety of authors who have commented upon Indian Jewry: from the first-century historian Josephus' (1888) comments about Indian philosophy, to the third-century Bishop Eusebius' (1959) mention of first-century missions to Indian Jews, to fourth-century St. Jerome's (1854) mention of Jewish trading outposts stretching from Ethiopia to India, to travellers Marco Polo (n.d.) and Ibn Battúta (1969), and to mystical messianists Moses 'Edrehi (1836) and Menasseh Ben Israel (1665).

In reading these incidental sources, one begins to appreciate the antiquity of Indian Jewry, of their importance in international trade during medieval times (Goitein 1967-83, Fischel 1968), and of the Jewish and Gentile world's fascination with the story of the ten lost tribes (Godbey 1930, Avihail and Brin 1985).

Adler, Elkan N., *Jews in Many Lands* (London, 1905). German version: *Von Ghetto Zu Ghetto* (Stuttgart: Strecker und Schroder, 1909). [German version contains material not found in original English edition.]

———, 'A Jewish Merchant in China at the Beginning of the Tenth Century,' in *Abhandlung Zur Erinnerung An H.P. Chajes* (Vienna, 1933): 1-5.

Ahir, D.C., *Dr. Ambedkar on Jews & Negroes* (New Delhi: Blumoon Books, 1998).

Ali, Maulana Muhammad, 'Jesus Among the Ten Lost Israelite Tribes in the East,' *Review of Religions* (Qadiyan, Punjab), (January 1903): 6-19, (February 1903): 51-66, (May 1903): 181-92, (June 1903): 220-5, (October 1903): 393-9.

Anonymous, 'Jews in Tibet,' *The Chinese Repository* (Canton) 2, 5 (1833): 237-8.

———, 'Une Tribu Juivre au Thibet,' *Bulletin Catholique de Pékin* 26, 107 (March 1929): 142-3.

———, *India and Palestine: A Reply by a Student of West Asian Affairs* (New Delhi: Society for Parliamentary Studies, 1967).

Aran, Yair, ed., *Indians and Israelis: A Story of Cooperation between Peoples* (Bombay: Wagle Process Studies, 1972).

Asaf, Simchah, 'From Egypt to Aden and India,' *Tziyon* 4, nos. 3/4 (Jerusalem, n.d.): 232-5. [In Hebrew.]

Ashtor, Eliyahu, *The Jews of Moslem Spain*, trans. from the Hebrew by Aaron Klein and Jenny Malchowitz Klein, 3 vols. (Philadelphia: Jewish Publication Society, 1984).

Asian-Pacific Jewish Association, *Asia-Pacific Survival Guide for the Jewish Traveller* (Melbourne: Asian-Pacific Jewish Association, n.d. 1988).

Ausubel, Nathan, *A Treasury of Jewish Folklore: Stories, Traditions, Legends, Humor, Wisdom and Folk Songs of the Jewish People* (New York: Crown Publishers, 1948).

Avihail, A., and A. Brin, *The Lost Tribes in Assyria* (Jerusalem: Amishav, 1985).

Avimor, Shimon, *Relations between Israel and Asian and African States: A Guide to Selected Documentation*, no. 6 *INDIA* (Jerusalem: Hebrew University, 1991).

———, *Relations between Israel and Asian and African States: A Guide to Selected Documentation*, no. 5 *UNION OF BURMA* (Jerusalem: Hebrew University, 1989).

Barbosa, Duarte, *A Description of the Coasts of East Africa and Malabar in the Beginning of the Sixteenth Century*, ed. Henry E.J. Stanley (New Delhi: Asian Educational Services, 1995).

Baron, Salmo Wittmayer, *A Social and Religious History of the Jews: High Middle Ages, 500-1200:* vol. III: *Heirs of Rome and Persia*

(New York and London: Columbia University Press, and Philadelphia: Jewish Publication Society, 1957).

———, *A Social and Religious History of the Jews: High Middle Ages, 500-1200:* vol. IV: *Meeting of East and West* (New York and London: Columbia University Press, and Philadelphia: Jewish Publication Society, 1957).

Basham, A.L., *The Wonder that Was India* (Calcutta: Rupa & Co., 1981).

Beazley, C. Raymond, 'Missions (Christian, Early and Mediaeval),' *Encyclopaedia of Religion and Ethics*, ed. James Hastings (New York: Charles Scribner's Sons, 1958 [repr.]): VIII: 705-12

Ben-Zvi, Itzhak, *The Exiled and the Redeemed* (Jerusalem: Yad Itzhak Ben-Zvi Publications, 1976 [Philadelphia: Jewish Publication Society, 1957]).

Bloch, Joshua, *Jewish Life in Oriental Countries: A List of Books and Manuscripts Exhibited at the New York Public Library, March 30th to December 31st, 1926* (New York: The New York Public Library, 1927).

Bornani, Eli, *A Historical Atlas of the Jewish People* (New York: Alfred A. Knopf, 1992).

Boulnois, L., *The Silk Road* (New York: E.P. Dutton, 1966).

Bowman, Steven, 'Review of Amitav Ghosh, *In An Antique Land* (1992),' *Journal of Indo-Judaic Studies* 2 (1999): 144-6.

Bridgeman, E.C., 'Jews in China: Notices of Those in the East by Josephus, Peristol, Benjamin of Tudela, Manasseh, and the Jesuits,' *The Chinese Repository* 3 (August 1834): 172-5.

Caroe, Olaf, *The Pathans 550 B.C.-A.D. 1957* (London: Macmillan & Co., and New York: St. Martin's Press, 1965).

Changqi, Chen, 'Buddhist Monk or Jewish Rabbi?,' in Sidney Shapiro, ed., *Jews in Old China: Studies by Chinese Scholars* (New York: Hippocrene Books, 1984): 139-42.

Christensen, Arthur, *L'Empire des Sassanides: Le Peuple, l'Etat, la Cour* (København: B. Lunos Bogtr., 1907).

Clavijo, G. Dem, *Embassy to Tamerlane, 1403-1406*, trans. from the Spanish by G. le Strange (New York and London: Harer & Br., 1928).

Cohen, Hayyim, and Zvi Yehuda, eds., *Asian and African Jews in the Middle East 1860-1971: An Annotated Bibliography* (Jerusalem: Ben-Zvi Institute, 1976).

Deshen, Shlomo, 'Anthropologists and the Study of the Cultures of Oriental Jews,' *Pe'amim* 1 (1979): 76-84. [In Hebrew.]

Ebenezer, Matthew, 'American Presbyterians and Islam in India, 1855-1923: A Critical Evaluation of the Contribution of Isidor Loewenthal (1826-1864) and Elwood Morris Wherry (1843-1927),' Ph.D. dissertation, Westminster Theological Seminary (Philadelphia), 1998, xiii, 345p. Abstracted in *Dissertation Abstracts International* (Ann Arbor, MI) 59, no. 5 (November 1998), p. 1717-A. UMI (formerly University Microfilms International) order number 9832798. [Loewenthal was a Polish Jew who converted to Christianity in the United States and worked in India as a missionary between 1855 and 1864.]

'Edrehi, Rev. Dr. Moses, *An Historical Account of the Ten Tribes, Settled beyond the River Sambatyon in the East, with Many Other Curious Matters Relating to the State of the Israelites in Various Parts of the World* (London: M. Edrehi, 1836).

Elazar, Daniel Judah, *The Other Jews: The Sephardim Today* (New York: Basic Books, 1989).

Eusebius, *The Ecclesiastical History, with an English Translation*, tr. Kirsopp Lake, 2 vols. (Cambridge, MA: Harvard University Press, and London: William Heinemann, 1959).

Farewell, Christopher, *An East-India Coalition* (Amsterdam: De Cappo, 1971 [1633]).

Fischel, Walter J., *Jews in the Economic and Political Life of Mediaeval Islam* (London: Royal Asiatic Society, 1968).

———, 'The Jews of Central Asia (Khorasan) in Medieval Hebrew and Islamic Literature,' *Historia Judaica* 7, 1 (April 1945): 29-50.

———, 'The Jews in Mediaeval Iran from the 16th to the 17th Centuries: Political, Economic, and Communal Aspects,' in Saul Shaked, ed., *Irano-Judaica: Studies Relating to Jewish Contacts with Persian Culture Throughout the Ages* (Jerusalem: Ben Zvi Institute, 1982): 265-91.

Flaum, Shulamit, *Wandering Daughter of Israel* (Jerusalem: Bet Mischar and Achiasaf, 1936). [In Hebrew.]

Gidney, W.T., *The History of the London Society for Promoting Christianity Amongst the Jews* (London: LSPCAJ, 1908).

Gil, Moshe, 'The Radhanite Merchants and the Land of Radhan,' *Journal of the Economic and Social History of the Orient* 17, 3 (1974): 299-328.

Glucklich, Ariel, 'Brahmins and Pharisees: The Roots of India's Anti-Zionism,' *Midstream* 34, 1 (1988): 12-15.

Godbey, Allen H., *The Ten Lost Tribes: A Myth—Suggestions Towards Rewriting Hebrew History* (Durham, NC: Duke University Press, 1930).

Goitein, Solomon D.F., *Jews and Arabs: Their Contacts Through the Ages* (New York: Schocken Books, 1974 [1955]).

———, *A Mediterranean Society: The Jewish Communities of the Arab World as Portrayed in the Documents of the Cairo Geniza*, 4 vols. (Berkeley and Los Angeles: University of California Press, 1967-83).

Goldsmid, *The Arguments Advanced against the Enfranchisement of the Jews* (London, 1833).

Gourgey, Percy Sassoon, *Ideals, India, Israel in Asia* (Bombay: Pillar, 1948).

Graetz, Solomon, *The History of the Jews*, vol. 1 (Philadelphia: Jewish Publication Society, 1891-8).

Hacohen, Dvora and Menachem, *One People: The Story of the Eastern Jews* (New York: Adama Books, 1986).

Hamilton, Alexander, *A New Account of the East Indies*, ed. Sir William Foster, 2 vols. (New York: DeCapo, and Amsterdam: N. Israel, 1970 [1727, 1744]).

Heine, Steven, 'Review of Richard Foltz, *Religions of the Silk Road* (1999),' *Journal of Indo-Judaic Studies* 4 (2001): 131-2.

Hertz, Joseph Herman, *The First Pastoral Tour to the Jewish Communities of the British Dominions by the Chief Rabbi* (London: H. Milford, 1924).

Hooper, J.S.M., *The Bible in India* (London: Oxford University Press, 1938).

Ibn Battúta, *Travels in Asia and Africa, 1325-1354*, trans. H.A.R. Gibb (New York: Augustus M. Kelley, 1969 [1929]).

James, Montague Rhodes, tr., 'The Acts of Thomas,' in *The Apocryphal New Testament, being the Apocryphal Gospels, Acts, Epistles, and Apocalypses* (Oxford: Clarendon Press, 1924): 364-438.

Japhet, M.D., and P.K. Rajiv, *The Arab Israel Conflict* (Bombay: Peace Publications, 1967).

Jerome, St., 'Epistola Ad Dardanum,' letter 129 in J.-P. Migne, ed., *Patrologiæ Cursus Completus, Seu Bibliotheca Universalis, Integra, Uniformis, Commoda, Oeconomica, Omnium ss. Patrum, Doctorum Scriptorumque Ecclesiasticorum* (Parisiis: Excudebatur et Venit apud J.-P. Migne, 1854): 1090-1107.

Josephus, *The Works of Josephus, with a Life Written by Himself*, trans. William Whiston, standard edition (New York: A.C. Armstrong, 1888): III, 334-42.

Karttunen, Klaus, 'On the Contacts of South India with the Western World in Ancient Times, and the Mission of the Apostle Thomas,' in Asko Parpola and Bent Smidt Hansen, eds., *South Asian Religion and Society* (London: Curzon Press Ltd., and Riverdale, MD: Riverdale Press, Scandinavian Institute of Asian Studies Monograph No. 11, 1986): 189-204.

Kashani, Reuben, *Jewish Communities of the Far East* (Jerusalem: Council of the Sephardi and Oriental Communities, 1982). [In Hebrew.]

Kayserling, Meyer, *Christopher Columbus and the Participation of the Jews in the Spanish and Portuguese Discoveries* (New York: Longmans, 1894).

Klimkeit, H.-J., 'Der Buddha Henoch: Qumran und Turfan,' *Zeitschfirt für Religions- und Geistesgeschichte* 32 (1980): 367-77.

Lamotte, Étienne, 'Les premières relations entre l'Inde et l'Occident,' *Nouvelle Clio* 5 (1953): 83-118.

Latham, R., trans., *The Travels of Marco Polo* (Middlesex: Penguin Books, 1958).

Mandelbaum, David G., *Society in India*, 2 vols. (Berkeley: University of California Press, 1970).

Margabandhu, C., 'Ancient Sea-Ports of South India, their Trade Relationship with the Western World during the First Century BC to the Second Century AD,' in B.N. Mukherjee et al., eds., *Sri Dinesacandrika Studies in Indology* (Delhi: Sundeep Prakashan, 1983): 185-202.

Menasseh Ben Israel, *To His Highness the Lord Protector of the Commonwealth of England, Scotland, and Ireland: The Humble Address of Menasseh Ben Israel, a Diviner and Doctor of Physic, in Behalfe of the Jewish Nation* (London, 1665).

Mishkowsky, Noiah, *Ethiopie, Yiden in Afrike un Asie* (Chicago: Morris Ceshinsky, 1936). [In Yiddish.]

Moses, Nissim, 'Jews in Goa,' *Kulanu* 11, no. 3 (Autumn 2004): 5, 9.

Nathan, Sir Matthew, *Jewish Travellers: Presidential Address to the Union of Jewish Literary Societies* (London, 1912).

Neubauer, A., 'Where are the Ten Tribes?' *Jewish Quarterly Review*, old series, I, (1889): 14-28; 95-114; 185-201; 409-23.

Patai, Raphael, 'India: Jews Black and White,' *The Vanished Worlds of Jewry* (New York, 1981): 173-86.

———, *Tents of Jacob: The Diaspora Yesterday and Today* (Englewood Cliffs, NJ: Prentice-Hall, 1971), esp. pp. 415-23.

———, 'Judaism in Asia and Northeast Africa,' in Mircea Eliade, ed., *The Encyclopedia of Religion* (New York: Macmillan, 1987): 8, 164-72.

Pearson, M.N., ed., *Spices in the Indian Ocean World* (Aldershot: Varorium, 1996).

Philo of Alexandria, *Works, English and Greek*, trans. F.H. Colson and G.H. Whitaker, 10 vols. (London: Heinemann, and Cambridge: Harvard University Press, The Loeb Classical Library, 1929-62), 5: ii: 56, 59; 6: 182; 8: 89; 9: 74, 93-6.

Poa, Arie, 'A Stranger's Testimony: Some of Jan Huygen van Linschoten's Views on and from Goa Compared with Portuguese Sources,' *Itinerario: International Journal on the*

History of European Expansion and Global Interaction (Leiden, Netherlands) 28, no. 2 (2004): 117-34.

Polo, Marco. *The Travels of Ser Marco Polo* (New York: Orion Press, n.d.).

Pissurlencar, Panduronga S.S., *Agentes da Diplomacia Portuguesa na India (Hindus, Muçulmanos, Judeus e Parses)*, *Documentos Coordenados Anatados e Prefaciados* (Goa: Imprensa Nacional, 1952): Chapter VII: Coge Abrahão, 'Agentes Judeus da Diplomacia Portuguesa,' pp. 551-61. [In Portuguese.]

Prakash, Om, *European Commercial Enterprise in Pre-Colonial India* (Cambridge: Cambridge University Press, 1998).

Rehatsek, E., 'The Holy Inquisition at Goa,' *The Calcutta Review* 72 (1881): 311-53.

Rhys Davids, Thomas William, *Buddhist Birth Stories; or, Jâtaka Tales* (London: Trübner & Co., 1880).

Roshwald, Mordecai, 'Marginal Jewish Sects in Israel,' *International Journal of Middle Eastern Studies* 4 (1973): 219-37, and 328-54.

Sassoon, David S.D., 'The History of the Jews in Basra,' *Jewish Quarterly Review* 17, 4 (April 1927): 407-69.

———, *A History of the Jews of Baghdad* (Letchworth, 1949).

———, *Ohel Dawid: Descriptive Catalogue of the Hebrew and Samaritan Manuscripts in the Sassoon Library, London*, 2 vols. (London: Humphrey Milford, 5692/1932).

Schmidt, Francis, 'Entre Juifs et Grece: Le Modele Indien,' in *L'Inde et l'imaginaire* (Paris: Editions de l'École des Hautes Études, Collection Purusartha, no. 11, 1988): 33-46.

Sharot, Stephen, 'Minority Situation and Religious Acculturation: a Comparative Analysis of Jewish Communities,' *Comparative Studies in Society and History* 16 (1974): 329-54.

Shulman, Frank Joseph, *Directory of Individuals Interested in the Jews and the Jewish Communities of East, Southeast and South Asia* (Carrollton, GA: published in cooperation with the Sino-Judaic Institute, March 1993).

Stavorinus, John Splinter, *Voyages to the East-Indies*, 3 vols. (London, 1798).

Stehly, R., 'Une citation des Upanishads dans Joseph et Aséneth,' *Révue d'Histoire et de Philosophie religieuses* 55, 2 (1975): 209-13.

Stillman, Norman A., *The Jews of Arab Lands: A History and Source Book* (Philadelphia: Jewish Publication Society, 1979).

Thapar, Romila, *A History of India* (Harmondsworth: Penguin Books, 1966).

Wahab, Colonel, *Colonel Wahab's Notes on the Jews Serving in the Bombay Army* (Bombay: Educational Societies Press, 1879).

Wheeler, J. Talboys, ed., *Early Travels in India (16th & 17th Centuries)* (Delhi: Deep, 1974).

Williams, Raymond Brady, *Religions of Immigrants from India and Pakistan: New Threads in the American Tapestry* (Cambridge: Cambridge University Press, 1988).

Wolf, Lucien, ed., *Menasseh ben Israel's Mission to Oliver Cromwell, Being a Reprint of the Pamphlets Published by Menasseh Ben Israel to Promote the Re-Admission of the Jews to England, 1649-1656* (London: Macmillan, 1901).

Yegar, M., 'Jewish Communities in the Far East,' *Sephardi World* 2 (1984): 11-19.

JEWISH TRAVELLERS' ACCOUNTS

Jewish visitors to India often recorded their encounters with Indian Jews, and some of their diaries are of exceptional value and reliability. Ludwig Sternbach's articles (1945 and 1946) provide an overview of Gentile as well as Jewish visitors to Indian Jewish communities. De Paiva's 1686 visit to Cochin (Amzalak 1923) was the community's most significant encounter with European Jews and reads exceptionally well. Three nineteenth-century visitors—Hillel (Hillel 1832 and Fischel 1973), Saphir (1866) and Reinman (1884)—left exceptional accounts, as did Bar-Giora (1954) and Cowan (1971) more recently. The accounts of Benjamin of Tudelah (Adler 1907 and Asher n.d.) and Benjamin (1863) are the least reliable.

Adler, Elkan N., *Jewish Travellers: A Treasury of Travelogues from 9 Centuries* (New York: Hermon Press, 1966 [London: George Routledge, 1930]).

Adler, Marcus Nathan, ed., *The Itinerary of Benjamin of Tudela: Critical Text, Translation and Commentary* (New York: Philipp Feldheim, repr. n.d. [1907]).

Amzalak, Moses Bensabat, ed., *Notisias dos Judeos de Cochin mandados por Mosseh Pereyra de Paiva* (Lisbon: Musea Commercial, 1923). [In Portuguese.]

Asher, A., tr. & ed., *The Itinerary of Rabbi Benjamin of Tudela* (New York: Hakesheth Publishing Co., n.d.).

Bar-Giora, Naphtali, *Travels in India* (Tel Aviv, 1954). [In Hebrew.]

Benjamin, Israel Joseph, *Eight Years in Asia and Africa from 1846 to 1855* (Hanover: J.J. Benjamin II, 1863).

———, *Acht Jahre in Asien und Afrika. Von 1846 bis 1855. . .* Mit vergl. Notizen aus Benjamin de Tudela. . . (Hanover: The author, 1858).

———, *Un An de Séjour aux Indes Orientales (1849-1850)* (Alger: Imprimerie Typographique de Dubos Freres, 1854).

Carlebach, Alexander, *India: A Traveller's Journal* (Tel Aviv: Ayanot, 1955). [In Hebrew.]

Carmel, Yosef, *With the Scattered in the East* (Jerusalem: Israeli Publishing Institute, 1960). [In Hebrew.]

———, *A rayzne tsu farsntoysene brider* (Tel Aviv: Y.L. Perets, 1959). [In Yiddish.]

Cohen, David, *Twenty Days in India* (Jerusalem: Am Oved, 1948). [In Hebrew.]

Cohen, Israel, *The Journal of a Jewish Traveller* (London: John Lane, 1925).

Cooper, Alanna E., 'India's Jewish Geography as Described by Nineteenth-Century Traveler David D'Beth Hillel,' *Journal of Indo-Judaic Studies* 7-8 (2004-5): 25-35.

Cowan, Ida G., *Jews in Remote Corners of the World* (Englewood Cliffs, NJ: Prentice-Hall, 1971).

Eisner, Herbert, 'Out of This World,' *Menorah Journal* 35 (1947): 203-11.

Eshkoly, A., *Sippur David Hareubeni*, 2 vols., Jerusalem, 1940. [In Hebrew.]

Fischel, Walter J., 'David D'Beth Hillel: An Unknown Jewish Traveller to the Middle East and India in the 19th Century,' *Oriens* 10, 2 (1957): 240-7.

———, 'A Hitherto Unknown Jewish Traveller to India: The Travels of Rabbi David D'Beth Hillel to India (1828-1832),' in Daniel Jeremy Silver, ed., *The Time of Harvest: Essays in Honor of Abba Hillel Silver on the Occasion of his 70th Birthday* (New York: Macmillan, 1963): 170-85.

———, *Unknown Jews in Unknown Lands: The Travels of Rabbi David D'Beth Hillel (1824-1832)* (New York: KTAV, 1973).

Funke, Phyllis Ellen, 'The Jewish Traveler: Bombay,' *Hadassah Magazine* (November 1986): 26-8.

Hillel, Rabbi De Beth, *Travels of Rabbi De Beth Hillel* (Madras: privately published, 1832).

Kahane, Abraham, *Sippur N'siat David Reubeni* (Warsaw, 1922). [In Hebrew.]

Levanon, Yosef, *The Jewish Travellers in the Twelfth Century* (Lanham, MD: University Press of America, 1980).

de Paiva, Mosseh Pereyra, *Notisias Dos Judeos De Cochin* (Amsterdam: House of Vry Levy, 1687). [In Portuguese.]

Reinman, Shlomo, *Masa'ot Shlomoh b'Eretz Hodu, Burman, v'Sinim* (Vienna: Schur, 1884). [In Hebrew.]

Saphir, Yaacov, *Ebn Sapir (Sapphire Stone)* (Lick: L. Silbermann, 1866). [In Hebrew.]

Sharet, Moshe, *Mishoot b'Asia (From experiences in Asia)*: (Tel Aviv: Dvir, 1958) (third edn.) [In Hebrew.] [Three months of travel on behalf of Israel to Japan, Hong Kong, Singapore, Malaya, Cambodia, Burma, India.]

Shoskes, H., *Mein Reizeh Arum der Velt* (*My Journey Around the World*). (Buenos Aires: Unzer Buch, 1951). [In Yiddish; seven chapters about Indian Jews in Calcutta, Bombay, Pakistan.]

Simon, A.I., 'Did Benjamin of Tudelah Visit Malabar?,' *The Jewish Advocate* (January 1945).

Sternbach, Ludwik, 'Jews in Mediaeval India as Mentioned by Western Travellers,' *Indian History Congress Proceedings* 8 (1945): 169-97.

———, 'India as Described by Mediaeval European Travellers: Jewish Dwelling Places,' *Bharatiya Vidya* n.s. 7, 1-2 (1946): 10-28.

SCHOLARLY STUDIES OF INDIAN JEWRY IN GENERAL

Due to the complexity of the topic, most valuable scholarly studies focus on one of India's Jewish communities. Nevertheless, there have been a few attempts at scholarly treatments of Indian Jewry as a whole. Most notable is Fischel's 1960 Hebrew work that ought to be translated into English. Other notable efforts are by Mendelssohn (1920), Rabinowitz (1952), Strizower (1962), Timberg (ed. 1986), Abraham (1989), Katz (2000) and Weil (2002).

Also included in this section is a philological study of Biblical Hebrew borrowings from Sanskrit and Tamil (Rabin 1966 and 1971), studies of Jewish trading patterns (Braslavsky 1942, Rabinowitz 1948; and most notably Goitein 1953, 1954 and 1973), the historical links between Aden's and India's Jews (Assaf 1939, Goitein 1975), the role of Indian Jews in the Indian independence movement (Gourgey 1988; Isenberg 1988), an examination of Gandhi and subsequent Indo-Israeli relations (Shimoni 1977), Indian Zionism (Fischel 1962), and portraits of such exceptional Indian Jews as Garcia de Orta (D'Esaguy 1937, Fischel 1956b), Abraham Navarro (Fischel 1956 and 1957), Mulla Ibrahim Nathan (Fischel 1958), Pedro Pereira (Fischel 1964) and Mordecai Hamburger (Hart 1937).

Abraham, Margaret, 'Ethnic Identity and Marginality: A Study of the Jews of India' (Ph.D. dissertation in Sociology, Syracuse University, 1989).

———, 'Marginality and Disintegration of Community Identity Among the Jews of India,' a paper read at the annual meeting of the American Academy of Religion, New Orleans, LA, 19 November, 1990.

———, 'Ethnic Identity and Marginality Among Indian Jews in Contemporary India,' *Ethnic Groups* 9 (1991): 33-60.

———, 'The Normative and the Factual: An Analysis of Emigration Factors Among the Jews of India,' *The Jewish Journal of Sociology* 33, 1 (June 1991): 5-19.

———, 'Marginality and Disintegration of Community Identity among the Jews of India,' in Nathan Katz, ed., *Studies of Indian-Jewish Identity* (New Delhi: Manohar, 1995): 175-99.

———, 'From India to Israel: A Sociological Analysis of Migration Factors among Indian Jews,' *Population Review* 39, 1 & 2 (1995): 74-87.

———, 'Ethnicity and Marginality: A Study of Indian Jewish Immigrants in Israel,' *South Asia Bulletin* 15, 1 (1995): 108-23.

Abrahams, Israel, 'Anglo-Judaica in the Catalogue of the British Museum Hebrew Manuscripts,' *Miscellanies of the Jewish Historical Society of England* (1925): 75-80.

Ali, M. Athar, 'Muslims' Perception of Judaism and Christianity in Medieval India,' *Modern Asian Studies* 33, 1 (February 1999): 243-55.

Amar, Ariella, and Ruth Jacoby, 'India,' in *Gathering of the Nation: Treasures of Jewish Art: Documenting an Endangerd Legacy* (Jerusalem: Keter, 1998): 106-15.

Anonymous, 'India and Pakistan,' *American Jewish Year Book*, vol. 52 (New York: The American Jewish Committee, 1951): 423-4.

———, 'Review of Nathan Katz, *Who Are the Jews of India?* (2000),' *Jewish Book World* (New York) 19, no. 1 (Spring 2001): 22.

———, 'Review of Nathan Katz, *Who Are the Jews of India?* (2000),' *Association of Jewish Libraries Newsletter* (Evanston, Ill) 20, no. 3 (February/March 2001): 10.

———, 'Review of Nathan Katz, *Who Are the Jews of India?* (2000),' *Jewish Book World* (New York) 19, no. 2 (Fall 2001): 53.

Assaf, Simcha, 'M'Mitsrayim l'Aden v'l'Hodu,' *Zion* 4, 3/4 (1939): 232-6. [In Hebrew.]

Astren, Fred, *The Jewish Book Printed in India* (Berkeley, CA: Judah L. Magnes Museum, 1993).

Ben-Ya'akov, A., 'Emissaries from Palestine in Babylonia, Kurdistan, India and China,' *Yerushalayim* 2, 5: 257-86. [In Hebrew.]

Bhattacharaya, Pratibhaa, 'Identity and Acculturation.' [Review of Nathan Katz and Ellen S. Goldberg, *Kashrut, Caste and Kabbalah*, 2005], *The Hindu* (Madras, 18 October 2005).

Blumenthal Rare Book and Manuscript Library, *The Jewish Printed Book in India: Imprints of the Blumenthal Rare Book and Manuscript Library* (Berkeley CA: Judah L. Magnes Museum, 2002).

Brafman, Opra, 'Field Work in India among the Jewish Communities: December 1982-February 1983,' *Muze'on Yisra'el [The Israel Museum Journal]* 4 (Spring 1985): 93-8.

Braslavsky, Joseph, 'Jewish Trade Between the Mediterranean and India in the Twelfth Century,' *Zion* 7 (1942): 135-9. [In Hebrew.]

Cernea, Ruth F., 'Review of Shalva Weil, ed., *India's Jewish Heritage: Ritual, Art and Life-Cycle* (2002),' *Journal of Indo-Judaic Studies* (Saskatoon) 7-8 (2004-5): 110-12.

Chakravarti, Ranabir, 'Reaching Out to Distant Shores: Indo-Judaic Trade Contacts (up to C.E. 1300).' Read at 'A View from the Margin: The State of the Art of Indo-Judaic Studies,' Oxford Centre for Hebrew and Jewish Studies, U.K., 2-6 July 2002.

Chalier-Visuvalinga, Elizabeth, 'Asie du Sud-Est,' in Geoffrey Wigoder and Sylvie Ann Goldberg, eds., *Dictionnaire Encyclopedique du Judaïsme* (Paris: Les Éditions du Cerf, 1993): 1433-42.

Cohen, Lawrence, 'Review of Nathan Katz, *Who Are the Jews of India?* (2000),' *Persimmon* (Summer 2001): 106-8.

Dan, Ben-Amos, 'Hebrew Parallels to Indian Folktales,' *Journal of the Assam Research Society* 15 (1961): 37-45.

Egorova, Iuliia Ivanovna, 'Istoki I puti formirovaniia evreiskikh obshchin v Indii,' *Vostok* (Russia) 1999, no. 3: 59-72. [The Origin and Ways of Formation of the Jewish Communities in India. On the Baghdadi, Bene Israel, and Cochin Jews.]

———, 'Jewish Themes in the Press in Independent India,' in Tudor Parfitt and Yulia Egorova, eds., *Jews, Muslims, and Mass Media: Mediating the 'Other'*) London and New York: Routledge Curzon, 2004): 93-106.

Elazar, Daniel J., 'A Political Leader in the Postwar Indian Jewish Community,' *Population Review* 39, 1 & 2 (1995): 95-7.

D'Esaguy, Augusto, 'Garçia Dorta and the Inquisition,' *Bulletin of the Institute of History of Medicine of Johns Hopkins University* 5 (1937): 483-7.

Falber, Mosheh, *Yahadut Hodu* (Yerushalayim: Misrad ha-hinukh veha-tarbut, Merkaz ha-hasbarah, 1990). [In Hebrew.]

Fischel, Walter J., 'The Region of the Persian Gulf and Its Jewish Settlements in Islamic Times,' in Saul Lieberman, ed., *Alexander Marx Jubilee Volume* (New York: Jewish Theological Seminary of America, 1950): 203-30.

———, 'Abraham Navarro-Jewish Interpreter and Diplomat in the Service of the English East India Company (1682-1692),' *Proceedings of the American Academy for Jewish Research* XXV (1956a): 39-62.

———, 'Leading Jews in the Service of Portuguese India,' *Jewish Quarterly Review* 47 (July 1956): 37-57.

———, 'Abraham Navarro-Jewish Interpreter and Diplomat in the Service of the English East India Company,' Part 2 in *Proceedings of the American Academy for Jewish Research* XXVI (1957): 25-39.

———, 'Mulla Ibrahim Nathan: Jewish Agent of the British During the First Anglo-Afghan War,' *Hebrew Union College Annual* 29 (1958): 331-75.

———, *Ha-Yehudim b'Hoddu* (Jerusalem: Ben Zvi Institute, 1960). [In Hebrew.]

———, 'The Jewish Merchant Colony in Madras (Fort St. George) during the Seventeenth and Eighteenth Centuries,' *Journal of the Social and Economic History of the Orient* 3 (1960): 78-107; 175-95.

———, 'Early Zionism in India,' *Herzl Year Book* 4, ed. Raphael Patai (New York: Herzl Press, 1962): 309-28.

———, 'Garcia de Orta — A Militant Marrano in Portuguese-India in the 16th Century,' *Salo Wittmayer Baron Jubilee Volume on the Occasion of His Eightieth Birthday*, English section vol. I (Jerusalem: American Academy for Jewish Research, 1974): 407-32.

———, 'Pedro Pereira, Jewish Merchant in Surat (India), 1686-1721,' in Meir Benayahu, ed., *Itzhak Ben-Zvi Memorial Volume: Studies and Texts on the History of the Jewish Communities in the East*, vol. 2 (Jerusalem: Ben-Zvi Institute in the Hebrew University, 1964): 247-62. [In Hebrew.]

———, 'The Indian Archives: A Source for the History of the Jews of Asia (From the Sixteenth Century On),' a paper read before the 4th World Jewish Congress of Jewish Studies, Jerusalem, July-August 1965.

———, 'The Present State of Research on the History of the Jews in India from the 16th Century On,' in Mishael Maswari Caspi, ed., *Jewish Tradition in the Diaspora: Studies in Memory of Walter J. Fischel* (Berkeley, CA: Judah L. Magnes Museum, 1981): 23-33.

Fischel, Walter J., Paul Gottlieb and Avigdor Herzog, 'India,' *Encyclopedia Judaica* (1972), vol. 8: 349-60.

Goitein, Solomon D.F., 'The Jewish India-Merchants of the Middle Ages,' *India and Israel* 6 (1953): 36-7.

———, 'From the Mediterranean to India,' *Speculum* 19, 2/1 (1954): 181-97.

———, 'Letters and Documents on the India Trade in Medieval Times, *Studies in Islamic History and Institutions* (Leiden, 1966).

———, *Letters of Medieval Jewish Traders* (Princeton: Princeton University Press, 1973).

———, 'Yahudut teman u-shar hodu ha-yehudi (Yemenite Jewry and the India Trade),' in Yisrael Yesha'yahu and Yosef Tobi, eds., *Yahadut teman (Jews of Yemen: Studies and Researches)* (Jerusalem: Yad Yitzhak Ben-Zvi, 1975): 47-69. [In Hebrew.]

———, 'From Aden to India,' *Journal of the Economic and Social History of the Orient* 23, I & II (1980): 43-66.

Gourgey, Percy S. 'India.' *American Jewish Year Book* (New York: The American Jewish Committee, vol. 54, 1953): 416-21.

———, 'Indian Jews and the Indian Freedom Struggle,' *Indo-British Review* 15, 1 (1988): 85-90.

———, 'Indian Jews and the Indian Freedom Struggle,' *Population Review* 39, 1 & 2 (1995): 88-94.

Hart, R.J. d'Arcy, 'The Family of Mordecai Hamburger and their Association with Madras,' *Miscellanies* (London) 3 (1937): 57-76.

Heredia, Rudolf C. 'The Jews of India,' *Contributions to Indian Sociology*, new series 34, no. 2 (May-June 2000): 283. [Review of Benjamin J. Israel, *The Jews of India*, 1998.]

Isenberg, Shirley Berry, 'Indian Nationalism and India's Jews,' *Indo-British Review* 15, 1 (1988): 91-110.

———, 'Indian Jewry in India and in Israel: A Brief Introduction,' *Population Review* 39, 1 & 2 (1995): 54-65.

Israel, Samuel, *Indian Book Publishing, 1947-1980: Contemporary Reviews and Appeals* (New Delhi: Mosaic Books, 2000).

Joseph-Witham, Heather Rose, 'Transforming Folk Beliefs: A Community of Indian Jews in Los Angeles and the Process of Believing,' Ph.D. dissertation, University of California at Los Angeles, 1998, xi, 236 p. Abstracted in *Dissertation Abstracts International* (Ann Arbor, MI) 58, no. 12 (June 1998), p. 4756-A. UMI (formerly University Microfilms International) order number 9817998.

Judah L. Magnes Memorial Museum, *The Jews of India Exhibit* (Berkeley: The Jewish Museum of the West, 1969).

Kashani, Reuben, *The Jewish Communities of India* (Jerusalem: Va'ed Idat Hasfardim, 1977). [In Hebrew.]

Katz, Nathan, 'Review of Thomas Timberg, *Jews in India* (1986),' *Journal of Asian Studies* 46, 1 (February 1987): 199-201.

———, 'Contacts between Jewish and Indo-Tibetan Civilizations through the Ages: Some Explorations,' *Tibet Journal* (special issue on 'Western Religions and Tibet,' ed. Nathan Katz), 16, 4 (Winter 1991): 90-109.

———, ed., *Studies of Indian-Jewish Identity* (New Delhi: Manohar, 1995).

———, *Who Are the Jews of India? Identity Balanced, Identity Transformed, Identity Aloof* (Berkeley, CA and London: University of California Press, 2000).

———, 'Review of Ken Blady, *Jewish Communities in Exotic Places* (2000),' *Journal of Indo-Judaic Studies* (Saskatoon) 4 (2001): 133-4.

———, 'Jewish Folklore' and 'Judaism,' in Peter J. Claus, Margaret A. Mills, and Sarah Diamond, eds., *South Asian Folklore: An Encyclopedia* (New York and London: Routledge, 2003): 309-10 and 313-14.

———, 'Review of Tudor Parfitt, *The Lost Tribes of Israel: The History of a Myth* (2002),' *Bulletin of the School of Oriental and African Studies* (London) 66, no. 2 (2003): 23-5.

———, 'Judaism: Judaism in Asia,' in Lindsay Jones et al., eds., *Encyclopedia of Religion,* 2nd edn. (Farmington Hills, MI, and New York: Macmillans Reference, 2005), vol. 7: 5004-11.

———, 'The Jews, Israel and India,' *Changing Jewish Communities*, Jerusalem Center for Public Affairs, no. 2, 15 November 2005: 1-14. [An interview with Dr. Manfred Gerstenfeld.]

Katz, Nathan and Ellen S. Goldberg, 'The Last Jews in India and Burma,' *Jerusalem Letter* (Jerusalem Center for Policy Studies 101) (15 April 1988): 1-8.

King, Noel Q., 'A Preliminary Note on Some Jewish Anglo-Indians,' in Mishael Maswari Caspi, ed., *Jewish Tradition in the Diaspora: Studies in Memory of Walter J. Fischel* (Berkeley, CA: Judah L. Magnes Museum, 1981): 191-6.

Malekar, Ezekiel Isaac, 'The Jewish Community in India and Their Personal Law,' *Religion and Society* 38, 1 (March 1991): 48-63.

Mendelssohn, Sidney, *The Jews of Asia, Especially in the Sixteenth and Seventeenth Centuries* (London: Kegan Paul, Trench & Trubner, 1920).

Musleah, Ezekiel N. "India." *American Jewish Year Book* (New York: The American Jewish Committee, vol. 62, 1961): 377-81.

Neumann, Stephanie, 'The Jews of India: A Study in Majority-Minority Relations' (M.A. thesis in Geography, New York University, June 1960).

Oppert, Gustav, 'Ueber die Jüdischen Colonien in Indien,' in George Alexander Kohut, ed., *Semitic Studies in Memory of Rev. Dr. Alexander Kohut* (Berlin: S. Calvary & Co., 1897): 396-419. [In German.]

Parfitt, Tudor, 'Lost Tribes in India,' in *The Thirteenth Gate: Travels among the Lost Tribes of Israel* (Bethesda, MD: Adler & Adler, 1987): 36-67.

———, 'Descended from Jewish Seed: Genetics and Jewish History in India — The Bene Israel and the Black Jews of Cochin,' *Journal of Indo-Judaic Studies* (Saskatoon) 6 (2003): 7-18.

———, *The Jews of Africa and Asia* (London: Minority Rights Group, MRG Report No. 76, n.d.): 8-9.

Pollack, Michael, 'Far Flung Jews,' *Congress Monthly* (February 1989): 18-19. [Review of Parfitt, *The Thirteenth Gate: Travels among the Lost Tribes of Israel* (1987).]

Rabin, Chaim, 'Rice in the Bible,' *Journal of Semitic Studies* 11 (Spring 1966): 2-9.

———, 'Loanword Evidence in Biblical Hebrew for Trade between Tamilnad and Palestine in the First Millennium B.C.,' *Proceedings of the Second International Seminar of Tamil Studies* (Madras: International Association of Tamil Research, 1971), I: 432-40.

Rabinowitz, Louis, *Jewish Merchant Adventurers: A Study of the Radanites* (London: Edward Goldston, 1948).

———, *Far East Mission* (Johannesburg: Eagle Press, 1952).

Reissner, H.G., 'Maimonides on India,' *India and Israel* (1948): 22-4.

———, 'The Jews of India,' *India and Israel* 1, 1 (July 1948): 12-13; and 1, 2 (August 1948): 14-15.

———, 'Indian-Jewish Statistics, 1837-1941,' *Jewish Social Studies* 12 (1950): 349-65.

———, 'Indian-Jewish Statistics 1837-1941,' *India and Israel* 3 (1951): 46-7.

Roland, Joan G., 'The Jews of India: Communal Survival or the End of a Sojourn?,' *Jewish Social Studies* XLII (1980): 75-90.

———, 'Jews,' in Ainslee T. Embree, ed., *Encyclopedia of Asian History* (New York: Charles Scribner's Sons, 1988): 2, 214-16.

———, *Jews in British India: Identity in a Colonial Era*, 2nd edn. (Hanover, NH: University Press of New England, 1989).

———, 'Adaptation and Identity among Second-Generation Indian Jews in Israel,' *Jewish Journal of Sociology* 37, no. 1 (1995): 5-37.

———, 'Jews in India Today: A Community Survives,' *Pe'amim* (September 1997). [In Hebrew.]

———, *The Jewish Communities of India: Identity in a Colonial Era*, 2nd edn. (New Brunswick, NJ: Transaction, 1998).

———, 'The Contribution of the Jews of India,' in Shalva Weil, ed., *India's Jewish Heritage: Ritual, Art, & Life-Cycle* (Mumbai: Marg Publications, 2002): 111-21.

———, 'Review of Nathan Katz, *Who Are the Jews of India?* (2000),' *Jewish Quarterly Review* 94, 3 (2004): 556-62.

Schermerhorn, R.A., 'Parsis and Jews in India: A Tentative Comparison' (n.d.): 119-22.

———, 'Jews: A Disappearing Minority,' in *Ethnic Plurality in India* (Tucson: University of Arizona Press, 1978): 238-61.

———, 'Jews without Middleman Status: Their Historic Position in China and India,' *Journal of Intercultural Studies* 2, 2 (1981): 5-21.

Sealy, J.-A., 'Qol Yhude Hoddu: A Study of the Liturgical and Semi-religious Music Traditions of Indian Jewry as now Practiced in Greater London,' Ph.D. dissertation, Goldsmiths' College, University of London, 1993. [Noted in Aslib., *Index to Theses with Abstracts Accepted for Higher Degrees by the Universities of Great Britain and Ireland*, vol. 44, part 1 (1995): 44-0517.

Sharma, Jagdish Saran, *India's Minorities: A Bibliographical Study* (Delhi: Vikas, 1975).

Sheskin, Ira M., 'Review of A. Bhende and R. Jhirad, *Demographic and Socio-Economic Characteristics of Jews in India* (1997),' *Journal of Indo-Judaic Studies* (Saskatoon) 2 (1999): 143-4.

Shimoni, Gideon, *Gandhi, Satyagraha and the Jews: A Formative Factor in India's Policy towards Israel* (Jerusalem: The Hebrew University, Jerusalem Papers on Peace Problems no. 22, 1977).

Sikand, Yoginder, 'Review of Nathan Katz, *Who Are the Jews of India?* (2000),' *Contemporary South Asia* 10, 27 (2001): 285-6.

Silliman, Jael, 'Review of Nathan Katz, ed., *Studies of Indian Jewish Identity* (1995),' *Journal of Asian Studies* 56, 1 (February 1997): 230-2.

Slapak, Orpa, *The Jews of India: A Story of Three Communities* (Jerusalem: Israel Museum, 1995).

Spinner, G., 'Review of Nathan Katz, *Who Are the Jews of India?* (2000),' *Choice* 38, 8 (April 2001): 415.

Strizower, Schifra, *Exotic Jewish Communities* (London and New York: Thomas Yoseloff, 1962).

———, 'The Jews in India,' *New Society* 9 (January 1964): 16-17.

Timberg, Thomas A., ed., *Jews in India* (New Delhi: Vikas and New York: Advent, 1986).

———, 'On Indian Jews,' in Timberg, ed., *Jews in India* (New Delhi: Vikas, 1986): 3-11.

Tourreil, Savithri de, 'Review Essay of Nathan Katz, *Who Are the Jews of India?* (2000),' *Journal of Religion and Culture* (Montréal) 14 (2000/1): 195-200.

Wallia, C.J.S., 'Who are the Jews of India?,' *IndiaPost* (20 June 2002): 55; Also in *IndiaStar Review of Books* [www.indiastar.com] (May 2002). [Review of Nathan Katz, *Who Are the Jews of India?* (2000).]

Warokner, Jay A., 'In Search of India's Synagogues: Their Architecture and History,' in Shalva Weil, ed., *India's Jewish Heritage: Ritual, Art, & Life-Cycle* (Mumbai: Marg Publications, 2002): 37-49.

Wasserstein, Bernard, 'Unchoosing People: Jewish Experiences in Europe and Asia,' *Times Literary Supplement* (London, 9 November 2001): 4-5. [Review essay of Nathan Katz, *Who Are the Jews of India?* (2000), among other works.]

Weil, Shalva, 'The Literature of the Jews in India,' in H. Jason, ed., 'The Folk Literature of the People of Israel,' *Indian Journal of Folkloristics* 3, 5/6 (1980): 68-71.

———, 'India, Zionism in' and 'Indian Jews in Israel,' in Geoffrey Wigoder, ed., *The New Encyclopedia of Zionism and Israel* (Cranberry, NJ: Associated University Presses, 1994): 651-3.

———, 'Remote Jewish Communities,' in Ely Ben-Gal, ed., *The People of the Menorah* (Tel Aviv: Maccabi World Union, 1995): 68-73.

———, 'Review of B.J. Israel, *The Jews of India* (1998),' *Journal of Indo-Judaic Studies* (Saskatoon) 4 (2001): 119-22.

———, 'The Jewish Communities of India,' in Avshalom Mizrachi and Aharon Ben-David, eds., *The Tribes — Evidence of Israel: Exile, Immigrations, Absorption, Contribution and Integration* (Netanya: Association for Society and Culture, Documentation and Research, 2001), 272-81. [In Hebrew.]

———, 'At Home in Exile,' *Biblio: A Review of Books* 4, nos. 9 & 10 (2001): 18-19.

———, *India, the Larger Immigration from Eastern Countries* (Jerusalem: Ben-Zvi Institute and Ministry of Education, 2001). [In Hebrew.]

———, ed., *India's Jewish Heritage: Ritual, Art, & Life-Cycle* (Mumbai: Marg Publications, 2002a).

———, 'The Heritage and Legacy of the Jews of India,' in Shalva Weil, ed., *India's Jewish Heritage: Ritual, Art, & Life-Cycle* (Mumbai: Marg Publications, 2002b): 9-21.

———, 'Judaism: South Asia,' in *Encyclopedia of Modern Asia* (New York: Scribner's, 2004).

Weinstein, Brian, 'Review of Nathan Katz, ed., *Studies of Indian Jewish Identity* (1995),' *Contemporary South Asia* 5, 2 (1996): 27-8.

———, 'Review of Orpa Slapak, ed., *The Jews of India: A Story of Three Communities* (1995),' *Journal of Indo-Judaic Studies* (Saskatoon) 1, 1 (1998): 99-102.

———, 'Biblical Evidence of Spice Trade Between India and the Land of Israel: A Historical Analysis,' *Indian Historical Review* (Delhi) 27, 1 (January 2000): 11-28.

———, 'Jewish Traders in the Indian Ocean — Tenth to Thirteenth Centuries: A Review of Published Documents from the Cairo Genizah,' *Journal of Indo-Judaic Studies* (Saskatoon) 4 (2001): 79-94.

———, 'Review of Nathan Katz, *Who Are the Jews of India?* (2000),' in *AJS Review* 27, no. 1 (April 2003): 126-8.

Wertheimer, Moshe, *On the Karaites and the Jews Who Are in India* (Jerusalem, 1962). [In Hebrew.]

White, Gregory, 'Review of Nathan Katz, *Who Are the Jews of India?* (2000),' *Conservative Judaism Quarterly* (2002): 92-4.

Wink, Andrew, 'The Jewish Diaspora in India: Eighth to Thirteenth Centuries,' *Indian Economic and Social History Review* 24, 4 (1987): 349-66.

Ya'ari, Abraham, *Hebrew Printing in the East* (Jerusalem: University Press, 1940). [In Hebrew.]

———, *Travels of a Safad Emissary in Eastern Lands* (Jerusalem: 1942). [In Hebrew.]

———, 'Emissaries from Israel in India,' *Sinai* 26 (1950). [In Hebrew.]

Zetlaoui, Monique, *Shalom India: histoire des communautés kiovres en Inde* (Paris: Imago, 2000).

POPULAR ACCOUNTS OF INDIAN JEWRY IN GENERAL

Of the comprehensive general interest accounts of Indian Jewry, the best is by Parasuram (1982). Others of note are by Japeth (1960), Elias and Isaac (1964, 1965), Chalier-Visuvalingam (1986/7), Sen (1989) and Katz and Goldberg (1989, 1990).

Indian synagogues are described by Eliya (1978), Kolet and Gadkar (1983, 1984) and Gadkar (1984). Missionary perspectives on Indian Jews include works by Buchanan (1911, 1912) and Grant (1959). Zionism in India is treated in Anonymous (1932), Gourgey (1957 and 1971) and Japeth (1970). Indian Jews who made *aliyah* are discussed by Koenig (1956) and Gourgey (1971). Other topics include Jews in the Indian military (Ashtamkar 1879) and in the Indian film industry (Benjamin 1965).

Abraham, A.S., 'The Jews of India,' *Illustrated Weekly of India* XC (Sunday, 19 October 1969): 8-11.

Adler, Elkan N., 'About the Indian Jews,' *Jewish Chronicle*, Parts I-IV, 5 October 1905; 11 May 1906; 1 June 1906; and 29 June 1906.

Ahmad, Irfan, 'The Jewish Hand: The Response of the Jamaat-e-Islami Hind,' in *Media, War, and Terrorism: Responses from the Middle East and Asia* (London and New York: Routledge/Curzon, 2004): 137-54.

Andrade, Carol, 'US Jews Shed Misconceptions on India Tour,' *Metropolitan* (6 December 1993): 1, 3.

Anonymous, 'A Symposium on the Indian Jewish Community,' in E. Elias & E. Isaac, eds., *Jews in India '64 with Who Is Who* (Ernakulam: Indo-Israel Publications, 1965): 58-66.

———, 'Zionism, Why is it so Lean in India?,' *Jewish Advocate* 3 (June 1932): 417.

———, 'India's Multi-racial Jewish Community Maintains a Close Alliance with Israel,' *Canadian Jewish News* (1 December, 1977).

———, 'Jew Terms Anti-Semitism Notably Scarce in India,' *India Abroad* (9 April 1982): 13.

———, 'Was Tagore a Jew and pro-Israel?,' *Statesman* (20 October 1991).

———, 'A Study On Hindu & Jewish Mysticism,' *News India* (29 November 1991): 20.

———, 'Indian Aliyah Eyed in Wake of Full Ties,' *New York Jewish Week* (7-13 February 1992): 16.

———, 'Feelings For Zionism Prompted Indian Jews To Go To Israel,' *News India-Times* (13 August 1993): 35.

———, 'Communities & Contributions-5: The Jews. *Shanwar Telis* and *Commodans*. The Sassoons,' *Mid-Day* (Bombay, 6 June 1995): 27.

———, 'Surveying and Documenting Jewish Art in India,' Hebrew University of Jerusalem, Center for Jewish Art, *Newsletter* 11 (November 1995): 14-18.

———, 'Jewish Contribution to Indian Freedom Struggle,' *India Weekly* (London, 31 January-6 February 1997): 2.

———, 'Nehru Helped Jewish Entry to India before WW-II,' UNI, (6 March 2004). http://www.newindpress.com/NewsItems.asp

Ashtamkar, Benjamin Samson, 'Preface' to *Colonel Wahab's Notes on Jews Serving in the Bombay Army* (Byculla: Education Society's Press, 1879). [Ashtamkar's translation into Marathi of Wahab's 12-page English text; Ashtamkar's 3-page preface in English.]

Association for the Study of Jewish Religion, *First Annual Report* (Poona, 1896).

Bar-Ilan, Meir, 'India and the Land of Israel: Between Jews and Indians in Ancient Times,' *Journal of Indo-Judaic Studies* (Saskatoon) 4 (2001): 39-77.

Bat Orn, Josefa, 'Odyssey Through Jewish India,' *Ammi* (World Union for Progressive Judaism, Shavout 1977): 4-5.

Beker, Avi, *Jewish Communities of the World* (Minneapolis: Lerner Publ. Co./World Jewish Congress, 1998).

Benjamin, Selim Elijah, 'The Jews in Indian Film Industry,' in E. Elias & E. Isaac, eds., *Jews in India '64 with Who Is Who* (Ernakulam: Indo-Israel Publications, 1965): 42-55.

Benjamin, Yehoshua [J.M.], *Mystery of the Lost Tribes* (New Delhi: Girija Printers & Publishers, 1989).

Berkson, Carmel, 'India: A Photo Story,' *Present Tense* 5, 3 (Spring 1978): 40-1.

Berman, Daphna, 'An unsung Jewish Community finally Writes its own History,' *Ha'aretz* (Tel Aviv, 5 January 2004). [About

Shalva Weil, ed., *India's Jewish Heritage: Ritual, Art, & Life-Cycle* (2003).]

Blady, Ken, 'Jewish Untouchables?,' in *Jewish Communities in Exotic Places* (Northvale NJ: Jason Aronson, 2000): 211-49.

Bookspan, Martin, 'The Eternal Light: From the Far Corners — Jews around the World: A Conversation with Elijah E. Jhirad,' N.B.C. Radio Network (New York: Jewish Theological Seminary of America, 12 January 1986).

Borden, Leslye, 'Kosher Gourmet: Indian Sephardic Feast a Healthy Treat,' *New York Jewish Week* (3-9 September 1993): 31ff.

Boykin, James H., *Black Jews: Ethiopia, India, United States* (Miami: James H. Boykin, 1982).

———, *Beta, Bene, and the Peripheral Diaspora* (Miami: James H. Boykin, 1889).

Brauner, David, 'India's Jewish Landscape,' *Jerusalem Post* (26 November 1998): 12.

Braustein, Susan L., 'Jews of India Exhibition Opens October 27,' *INS/MI* (November 1985): 3.

Brenner, Frédéric, *Les Juifs de l'Inde: exposition de photographies de Frédéric Brenner du 12 mai au 30 juin 1985 (prolongation jusqu'au 28 juillet 1985). A Musé d'art juif de Paris* (Paris: Musé d'art de Paris, 1985).

Buchanan, Claudius, *Christian Researches in Asia* (London: Society for the Promotion of Popular Instruction, 1911).

———, *The Works of the Reverend Claudius Buchanan, LL.D., comprising his Christian Researches in Asia; with Notices of the Translation of the Scriptures into the Oriental Languages* (Boston: Samuel T. Armstrong, 1812).

Chalier-Visuvalingam, Elizabeth, 'Connaissez-vous les Juifs Indiens?' *Les Nouveaux Cahiers* 87 (Hiver 1986-7): 16-22.

Daniel, Erna, and Sam Daniel, 'Issues Facing Indian Jewry Today and in the Millennium,' *Kulanu* 6, no. 4 (Winter 1999-2000): 5. [Letter.]

Devidayal, Samita, 'Jewish Educationist Felicitated,' *Times of India* (28 February 1992).

Dodd, D. Aileen, 'Lessons of Indian Jews Revealed,' *Herald* (Miami, 12 October 2000): 3B.

DuBow, Jodi Bodner, 'India Ink,' *Jewish Week* (New York, 17 March 2000): 30.

Elias, E., and E. Isaac, eds., *Jews in India with Who Is Who 1963* (Ernakulam: Indo-Israel Friendship Publications, 1964).

———, *Jews in India '64 with Who Is Who* (Ernakulam: Indo-Israel Publications, 1965).

Elijah, Samuel H., 'India's First Biblical Issue,' *JPJH* (September 1975): 1462.

———, 'Letter to the Editor,' *JPJH* (n.d.): 2395.

———, 'Letter to the Editor,' *Judaica Post—Journal of Philatelic Judaica* (n.d.): 607-8.

Eliya, Ben Eliahu, *The Synagogues of India* (Kiryat Motzkin: Eliahu Publishers, 1978).

———, *Indian Jewry* (Haifa: Ben Eliahu, 1984).

———, *Indian Jewry 1985-86* (Haifa: Beit Eliahu v'Leah, n.d.). [Rev. edn. of *Jews in India' 64*.]

Emanuel, Pinhas, *Indian Jewish Year Book* (Bombay: Abi Emu Publishers, 1969).

Ezekiel, I.A., 'A Miracle of Survival,' *India and Israel* 1, 5 (November 1948) and 1, 6 (December 1948).

Feldman, Stacy, and Maia Shiran, 'Jews in the Crown,' *Jerusalem Report* 11, no. 3 (5 June 2000): 53.

Fishel, John, 'Holding On: The Glory Days of India's Jews may be over but the Community maintains a Proud Presence,' *Jewish Journal* (6-12 October 1995): 17-18.

Forward, Martin, 'Jews and Parsees: Refugees in South Asia,' *Areopagus* (Arhaus, Denmark, Easter 1994): 13-16.

Gadkar, Daniel Elijah Benjamin, 'Synopsis of Synagogues in India and Pakistan,' in E.M. Jacob (Gadkar), ed., *The Religious and Cultural History of the Bene Israels of India* (1984): 11-15.

Gandhi, Indira, 'Great Heritage,' in Sattu S. Koder, ed., *Commemoration Volume* (1972): 5-8.

Gehlaut, Dharmvir, 'Maintaining Their Culture, Indian Jews Thrive in Israel,' *News India-Times* (New York, 22 December 2000): 12.

Ghosh, Amitav, *In An Antique Land* (Delhi: Ravi Dayal Publisher, 1992). [A novel.]

Gould, Lark Ellen, 'Jewish Masala: The Diverse Customs and Communities of the Dwindling Jews of India,' B'nai B'rith *International Jewish Monthly* (June-July 1993): 8-14.

Gilbert, Martin, *Letters to Auntie Flori* (New York: Schocken, 2002):

Gourgey, Percy S., 'Zionism in India,' *The Jewish Chronicle Supplement* (London, 30 August 1957).

———, ' Gandhi and the Jews,' in E. Elias & E. Isaac, eds., *Jews in India with Who Is Who 1963* (Ernakulam: Indo-Israel Publications, 1964): 46-8.

———, 'Zionism in India,' in R. Patai, ed., *Encyclopaedia of Zionism and Israel* (New York: Herzl Press, McGraw-Hill, 1971): 540-2.

———, 'Indian Jews in Israel,' in R. Patai, ed., *Encyclopaedia of Zionism and Israel* (New York: Herzl Press, McGraw-Hill, 1971): 542-3.

———, 'Indian Jews and the Indian Freedom Struggle,' *India Weekly* (London) (31 May-6 June 1991).

Grant, John Webster, *God's People in India* (Toronto: Ryerson Press, 1959).

Guo, Sung Lee, 'Sinew-Pluckers, Blowfish and Jewtown: Judaica Philately in the Far East,' *The Israel Philatelist* 39, 11/12 (December 1988): 5576-9.

Gupta, Ravinder K., 'Indian Secularism? Ask The Jews of India,' *News India* (8 January 1993): 54. (Letter to the editor.)

Harber, Kent, 'Indian Jews Establish 2 Temples,' *India Abroad* (1 January 1982): 2, 17.

Hostein, Lisa, 'Indian Jewry: A Tiny Tile in a Vast Mosaic,' *Philadelphia Jewish Exponent* (22 April 1994): 36-9.

Hyman, Mavis, *Indian-Jewish Cooking* (London: The Author, 1993).

Jacob, Elijah, Reuben Samuel, and Leora Ezekiel, *Jewish Landmarks in Bombay City* (Bombay: Jewish Religious Union Youth Group Publication, 1986/92).

Jacob, Ezekiel M.A. (Gadkar), 'Judaism and the Indian Ethos,' *Ohr* 30 (September 1991): 20-5.

———, 'Love for Zion,' *Indo-Israel Review* 30, 6 (March 1992): 2-4.

Japeth, Maurice David, *The Jews of-India: A Brief Survey* (Bombay: The Author, 1960).

———, 'Zionism in India,' (Poona) *Shalom* (September-October 1970): 1-3.

Jewish Welfare Association, Delhi and Northern India, *Reports* (New Delhi: 1955-7).

Jhirad, Ralphy, 'The Bene Israel, Cochini and Baghdadi Jewish Communities of India,' *Torchlight* (Spring 2004/5764): 10-11.

Kahn, Larry, '6,000 Jews & Counting: India's Jews Struggle to Survive,' *Manhattan Jewish Sentinel* (19 January 1994): 1, 6-7.

Katz, Nathan, 'Jews Once Flourished in India, Pakistan,' *Jewish Star Times* (Miami, 21 November 2001): 20.

Katz, Nathan, and Ellen S. Goldberg, 'Farewell to India,' *Points East: Journal of the Sino-Judaic Institute* 4, 1 (February 1989): 8-12.

———, 'Shalom, India,' *India* (March 1990): 10-17. [Photographs by E.S. Goldberg.]

Klass, Irene, 'East Meets West at Sephardic Congregation of Long Beach,' *Brooklyn Jewish Press* (20 April 1990): M30-1.

Klein-Halevi, Yossi, 'India's Jews: Meet the Castes,' *Moment* (June 1986): 36-44.

Koenig, Samuel, 'East Meets West in Israel,' *Phylon* 17, 2 (1956): 167-71.

Kolet, Ezra, and Daniel Elijah Benjamin Gadkar, *List of Synagogues and Prayer Hall in South Asia (India, Burma and Pakistan)* (New Delhi: Jewish Welfare Association and Centre for Jewish & Inter-Faith Studies, Bulletin No. 11, 1983).

———, *List of Synagogues and Prayer Hall in South Asia (India, Burma and Pakistan)* (New Delhi: Jewish Welfare Association and Centre for Jewish & Inter-Faith Studies, Bulletin No. 11, 2nd edn. 1984). [Revised, rpt. 1995.]

Kumaraswamy, P.R., 'In Memoriam: M.L. Sondhi,' *Journal of Indo-Judaic Studies* (Saskatoon)7-8 (2004-5): 120-2.

Leiter, Robert, 'Letter from Delhi: My Passage to India,' *Forward* (9 March 1996): 1, 13. [Reprinted, *Points East* 11, 3 (November 1996): 14.]

Levenson, Gabe, 'Winter in India,' *New York Jewish Week* (6-12 September 1991): 24, 55. [Letter to the editor: Elijah Jhirad, 'Disservice to Tradition' (11-17 October 1991): 23.]

Lobell, Richard, 'The Jews of India: Ghostly Echoes,' *Israel Today* (13 September 1985): 8.

———, 'The Jewish Community of India,' *WJC Report* 20, 3 (April-May 1996): 12-13.

Lottman, Herbert R., 'The Last Indian Jews,' *Present Tense* 3, 4 (Summer 1976).

Marks, Copeland, *Sephardic Cooking: 700 Recipes Created in Exotic Sephardic Kitchens from Morocco to India* (New York: Donald I. Fine, Inc., 1991). [Contains 30 recipes from Calcutta Jews, 19 from Bene Israel and 19 from Cochin.]

Mashyof, Shmuel Meir, *B'tochachi Yerushalayim: Mazchronotev shel Shemuel Meir Mashyof (1995-1973)* (Jerusalem, 1974), 'B'artzot HaMizrach Karahoq,' pp. 86-115. [In Hebrew.]

Matlock, Gene D., *Jesus and Moses are Buried in India!* (Adelanto, CA: Geo-Mind Publications, 1991).

Matthews, Veena, 'Still the Wandering Jew?,' *Sunday Times of India* (15 December 1991).

May, Sister, CSMV, *The Hope of Israel* (Delhi: ISPCK, 1969).

Mehra, Renu, 'India Nurtured Jewish Heritage Without Prejudice,' *India Worldwide* 1, 7 (February 1988): 7-9 and 35.

Menon, Harish C., 'Jews, the Lost Tribe of Indian Cinema,' *IndiaGlitz* (14 December 2005).

Moses, Joseph, 'Mayor Koch Honors Jews of India: City Hall Hanukkah Candle Lighting Ceremony,' *Kol Bina* 7, 2 (1989): 1-2.

Musleah, Rabbi Ezekiel N., 'India's Jewish Communities and Their Ties to Israel,' *Jewish Exponent* (Philadelphia, 26 April 1974).

Musleah, Rahel, 'ORT India is Family to the Country's Jews,'

Reporter: *Women's American ORT* 47, 3 (Fall 1997): 31-4.

Noronha, Percival, 'Jews in Goa,' in J.M. Benjamin, ed., *Jews of Cochin, India* (New Delhi: Jewish Welfare Association, 1999): 28-34.

Padiyath, Bhavama, 'Jews in India Make a Fascinating Topic of Study,' *Metropolitan* (2 December 1993).

Palnitkar, Milind, 'Jews Celebrate Indo-Israel Ties,' *News India* (6 March 1992): 18.

Parasuram, T.V., *India's Jewish Heritage* (New Delhi: Sagar Publications, 1982).

Peck, Arlene G., 'Indians Thriving in Israel,' *National Jewish Post & Opinion* (15 September 1993): 13-14.

Pezarkar, Elijah Solomon, *Jews in China and India* (Bombay, 1900).

Pratapan, B., Quaied Najmi, and V. Shankar Aiyar, 'A Time of Joy for Indian Jews,' *Indian Express Sunday Magazine* (16 February 1992): 1.

Provizer, Stephen, 'Local Architect Unravels History of Indian Jewry,' *Boston Jewish Advocate* (28 May-3 June 1993).

Ramanann, Sumana, 'Shalom Shabbath, Shalom,' *Outlook* (6 August 1997): 46-50.

Rassaby, Maurice, 'The Future of the Jews in India,' *Jewish Advocate* 13 (April 1944): 24.

Ronnen, Meir, 'The Jews in the Crown: Nearly Two Millennia of Jewish Presence in India are Summed up in a Colorful New Israel Museum Exhibition,' *Jerusalem Post International Edition* (3 August 1995): 16-17. [Reprinted in *Blitz* (Bombay, 9 September 1995): 11-12.]

Roth, Joan, 'The Four Corners,' *Forward* (New York, 29 April-2 July 1993). [Photography series about Indian Jews.]

Sastri, P.S., 'A Powerful Israel: An Asset to India: A New Federation Proposed,' in E. Elias & E. Isaac, eds., *Jews in India with Who Is Who 1963* (Ernakulam: Indo-Israel Publications, 1964): 74-7.

Scheinberg, Sy, 'The Jews of India,' in Karen Primack, ed., *Jews in Places You Never Thought Of* (New York: KTAV, 1998): 14-24.

Sen, Rehena, 'Shalom Delhi,' *Darshan* 6, 2 (February 1989): 7-10.

Sengupta, Shivaji, 'Delights of Jewish Kitchen,' *India Abroad* (2 July 1993): 34. [Review of Mavis Hyman, *Indian Jewish Cooking* (1993).]

Shenoy, Ramnath, 'Indian Jewish Population Drops but the Flame Burns,' *Maharashtra Herald* (29 August 1995).

Shohet, A.E., 'Gandhi and the Jews,' *The Jewish Advocate* (2 December 1938): 2-4. [Reprinted in Shimon Avimor, *Relations between Israel and Asian and African States: A Guide to Selected Documentation,* No. 6 *INDIA* (Jerusalem: Hebrew University, 1991): 35-8.]

Singh, George H., *Israel: The Study of the Jews from 2000 B.C. to 1970 A.D., and an Epilogue on the Years 1971-73* (Delhi: ISPCK-LPH, 1973).

Singh, Richa, 'Emigration Leads to Dwindling Jewish Population,' *India Abroad* (1 July 1997): 6.

Sitrin, Gregg, 'Rabbi Avihail's Amishav Seeks Out Lost Hebrews in the World's Remote Regions,' *United Israel Bulletin* 45, 3 (Winter 1990-1/Kislev 5751).

'Solomonides' [Elijah Solomon], 'Jews in China and India,' *Jewish Comment* 11, 1 (5, 12, 19 & 26 October 1900).

Spector, Johanna, 'Jews in India,' *Darshan* 5 (August 1983): 35-8.

———, 'The Jews of India,' *New India Digest* 54 (September-October 1996): 9-12.

Strauss, Eli, 'A Journey to India,' *Zion* 4 , 3-4 (1939): 217-31. [In Hebrew.]

Suri, Sanjay, 'On Indian-Jewish Cuisine,' *India Abroad* (2 July 1993): 34. [Review of Mavis Hyman, *Indian Jewish Cooking* (1993).]

Swamy, Subramaniam, 'The Secret Friendship between India and Israel,' *Sunday* (28 November-4 December 1982): 18-23.

Swet, Gershon, 'Goa und der Jude aus Posen—Ein Gespräch mit dem Orientalisten Walter Fischel,' *Aufbau* (26 January 1962): 32.

Szolgyemy, Blaise, 'Photo Essay: Out of India—The Jews of the Subcontinent,' *Lifestyles* 22, 123 (5753/1993): 48-9.

Tempest, Rone, 'Days Are Numbered for Jews of Cochin in India,' *Los Angeles Times* (29 March 1986): I-A-6.

Thayil, Jeet, 'Discussion on "Jews in the Cradle of India",' *India in New York* (14 April 2000): 23.

———, 'Acculturation nor Assimilation for India's Jewish Community,' *India Abroad* (New York, 18 December 2000): 51. [Review of Nathan Katz, *Who Are the Jews of India?* (2000).]

Tilak, Shrinivas, 'India and Israel at 50: In Search of a Composite Identity,' *Pragati—Montreal* 14, 4 (April-May 1998): 1, 3.

Tugend, Tom, 'Indian Jewry Struggling to Survive as Numbers Decrease,' *Jewish Chronicle* (28 January 1994): 7.

———, 'Passage to India: We visit the Jewish Community there and Discover a Dwindling Population Trying to Hold On,' *Los Angeles Jewish Journal* (4-10 February 1994): 20-2.

———, 'Indian Jews Predict the End of Their Millennium,' *Jerusalem Post* (21 February 1994): 7. [Reprinted in *Points East* 10, 1 (March 1995): 1, 3-4.]

———, 'Long History of Indian Jewry Dwindles,' *OJC* ('Ohio Jewish Courier') (24 March 1994): 27.

Ved, Mahendra, 'Slow and Steady: Growing Security Ties with Israel,' *Pragati—Montreal* 14, 4 (April-May 1998): 3.

Weil, Shalva, 'In Memoriam: J.B. Segal,' *Journal of Indo-Judaic Studies* 7-8 (2004-5): 117-19.

Weisz, Vera, 'Jewel in the Promised Land: They made Aliya quietly and Successfully. Today, Indian Jews are Fighting to Preserve Their Heritage,' *Jerusalem Post*, International Edition (24 July 1993): 10-11. [Reprinted as 'Passage From India,' *Points East* 10, 1 (March 1995): 1, 5-7.]

——— 'Jews of India: A Perfect Example of Tolerance,' *News India-Times* (13 August 1993): 34.

Wyenn, Than R., 'Passage to India's Jews,' *Los Angeles Jewish Community Bulletin* (31 January 1985).

Yehudi, Adv. Prem Doss S., *Israel as Seen by an Indian* (Trivandrum: The Author, 1983).

———, 'Israel: A View from India,' *New Swatantra Times* 2, 4 (June 1988): 10-12.

———, 'Tying the Bond of 3,000 Years,' *Jewish Telegraph* (Friday, 9 September 1988).

———, 'Focus on Beyth HaMikhadash,' *Ohr* 25 (November 1988): 5-8.

———, 'Tying the Bond of 3,000 Years,' *Kol Bina* 7, 1 (April 1989): 15-19.

CHAPTER 2

The Cochin Jews

PRIMARY DOCUMENTS AND MEMOIRS

Cochin historical texts include: Rahabi 1790 (trans. Koder 1949), Roby (aka Rahabi) 1911, 1939, Sarphati's undated synagogue record book, Salem 1913-59, 1929, 1972, and Simon 1947.

Among our most valuable—and charming!—sources are Hebrew accounts of visits by de Paiva in 1686 (Amzalak 1923), Sapir (1984) and Reinman (1984). The latter two were translated by I.S. Hallegua of Cochin, but English versions have yet to be published.

Finally, Eliya (n.d.) has culled some intriguing documents from government archives, and al-Din (1833) offers a Muslim view of the Jewish-Muslim struggles over Cranganore.

al-Din, Zain (Zeen-ul-deen), *Tohfut-ul-mujahideen*: *An Historical Work in the Arabic Language*, tr. Lt. M.J. Rowlandson (London: Oriental Translation Fund, 1833).

Amzalak, Moses Bensabat, ed., *Notisias dos Judeos de Cochin mandados por Mosseh Pereyra de Paiva* (Lisbon: Musea Commercial, 1923). [In Portuguese.]

Daniel, Ruby, assisted by Barbara C. Johnson, 'Memories of a Cochin Jewish Woman,' *Manushi* 67 (1990): 30-7.

———, 'Memories of Another Generation: The Saga of a Cochin Jewish Woman,' *India News* 33, 6 (15 March 1994): 8-9.

———, and Barbara C. Johnson, *Ruby of Cochin: An Indian Jewish Women Remembers* (Philadelphia: Jewish Publication Society, 1995).

Eliya, Ben Eliahu, *Cochin Jewish Records from State Archives* (Haifa: Eliahu Publishers, n.d.).

Kahane, Abraham, *Sippur N'siat David Reubeni (Diary of David Reubeni's Travels)* (Warsaw, 1922). [In Hebrew.]

Koder, S.S., 'A Hebrew Letter of 1768 [by Ezekiel Rahabi],' *Journal of the Rama Varma Archaeological Society* 15 (1949): 1-6.

Rahabi, David, *HaSefer Ohel David* (Amsterdam: Proops, 1791). [Study of Jewish, Muslim and Hindu calendars, in Hebrew.]

Rahabi, Ezekiel, 'Letter of 1768.' [Published in Hebrew by Naphtali Herz Wesseley, *Ha-Meassef*, Koeningsberg, 1790, vol. VI: 129-60; in abridged English translation by S.S. Koder in *Journal of the Rama Varma Archaeological Society*, 1949, vol. XV: 1-6.]

Reinman, Shlomo, 'Masa'oth Shlomo b'Kogin,' in S. Weil, ed., *MiKotsin l'Eretz Yisroel* (Jerusalem: Kumu Brinah, 1984): 31-9. [In Hebrew.]

Reubeni, David, *Sippur David Reubeni (Diary of David Reubeni)*, ed. Aaron Z. Eshkoly (Jerusalem, 1940). [In Hebrew.]

Roby, Naphtali E., *Divre Y'mei HaYehudim be Cochin* (Hebrew mss., Sassoon no. 268, Cochin, 1911).

———, *Eternal Light or Jewtown Synagogue* (Ernakulam: S.D. Printing Works, 1929).

———, *Toldot Beit Rahabi be Cochin* (Hebrew mss., in Judah Magnes Museum, Berkeley, CA, Cochin, 1939).

Salem, Avraham Baruch, *Personal Diaries* (unpublished mss., Judah Magnes Museum, Berkeley, CA, 1913-59).

———, *Cochin Jew Town Synagogue* (Haifa: Eliahu Publishers, 1972).

Samuel, Jacob, *Journey of the Missionary Labours of the Rev. Jaboc Samuel: Among the Jews at Cochin, during a Residence there of Five Months in 1834* (no place: no publisher, 1834).

Sapir, Yaacov, 'HaYehudim b'Kogin,' in S. Weil, ed., *MiKotsin l'Eretz Yisroel* (Jerusalem: Kumu Brinah, 1984): 21-30. [In Hebrew.]

Simon, A.I., *Songs of the Jews of Cochin* (Cochin: Archaeological Society of South India, 1947). [English and Malayalam.]

———, 'The Songs of the Jews of Cochin and their Historical

Significance,' *Bulletin of the Rama Varma Research Institute* (Trichur) 13 (1947).

Tavim, José Alberto Rodrigues daSilva, 'Os Judeus e a Espansão na India durante o Séulo XVI. O Exemplo de Isaac do Cairo Espiznao,'Lingua' e; Judeu de Cochim de Cima,' *Arquivos de Centro Cultural Calouste* (Paris, vol. XXXIII, 1994): 167-87.

Taylor, Ron, 'The White Jews of Cochin,' in Natasha Lehrer, ed., *The Golden Chain: Fifty Years of the Jewish Quarterly* (London, and Portland OR: Valentine Mitchell, 2003): 153. [Poem by Taylor written during the Winter of 1994-5.]

Yeates, Thomas, *Collation of a Hebrew Pentateuch; with preliminary remarks; containing an exact description of the manuscript and a notice of some others (Hebrew and Syriac) collected by Claudius Buchanan, in the year 1806, and now deposited in the Public Library, Cambridge; also a collation and description of a Ms. roll of the Book of Esther; and a Megillah of Ahasuerus, from the Hebrew copy originally extant in brazen tablets at Goa on the Malabar Coast, with an English translation* (Cambridge: Cambridge University Press, 1812).

INCIDENTAL REFERENCES/RELATED SUBJECTS

To understand the Cochin Jews entails an appreciation of their cultural context in Kerala. While there are many gaps in our knowledge of the southwestern state, the best studies are by Narayanan (1972), Pillai (1970), Logan (1981) and Menon (1984a and 1984b).

In particular, studies of Kerala's trade with the Middle East are important. The best is by Dasgupta (1967); other valuable works include those by Dasgupta and Pearsons (1987), Kusuman (1987), Bouchon (1988), Subrahmanyam (1990), and Chakravarti (2002).

Whiteway (1967) offers the best survey of the Portuguese period, Moens (1984) has first-hand accounts of the Dutch era, and Venn (1951) and Lawson (1860) have useful accounts of the Cochin Jews during the British period.

Some studies of Kerala Christianity that provide useful information about the Cochin Jews are: Thomas (1924), Ayyar (1926), Hooten (1930), Brown (1956), Firth (1961), Hunt (1968) and Mathew (1986). Unfortunately works relating Judaism with Islam and with Hinduism in Kerala are much rarer. Cherian (1969) and Friedmann (1975) deal with Islam and Iyer (1909, 1912) treats Hinduism in ways useful for approaching the Cochin Jews.

Aiyappan, A., 'Racial Minorities,' in S.S. Koder et al., eds., *Commemoration Volume* (Cochin: The Kerala History Association and The Cochin Synagogue Quatercentenary Celebration Committee, 1971): 211-24.

Anonymous, 'Grant to the Early Christian Church in India,' *Journal of the Royal Asiatic Society* 7 (1843): 343-4.

Ayyar, Rao Bahadur L.K. Anantakrishna, *Anthropology of the Syrian Christians* (Ernakulam: Cochin Government Press, 1926).

Bouchon, Geneviève, 'Sixteenth Century Malabar,' in Ashin Dasgupta and M.N. Pearson, eds., *India and the Indian Ocean 1500-1800* (Calcutta: Oxford University Press, 1987): 162-84.

———, *'Regent of the Sea': Cannanore's Response to Portuguese Expansion, 1507-1528*, trans. from the French by Louise Shackley (Delhi: Oxford University Press, 1988).

Bouchon, Genevieve, and Denys Lombard, 'The Indian Ocean in the Fifteenth Century,' in Ashin Dasgupta and M.N. Pearson, eds., *India and the Indian Ocean 1500-1800* (Calcutta: Oxford University Press, 1987): 46-70; esp. pp. 62-4.

Brown, Leslie Wilfred, *The Indian Christians of St. Thomas* (Cambridge: Cambridge University Press, 1956).

Burnell, A.C., 'On Some Pahlavi Inscriptions in South India,' *The Indian Antiquary* 3 (1874): 308-16.

Chakravarti, Ranabir, *Trade and Traders in Early Indian Society* (New Delhi: Manohar, 2002).

Cherian, A., 'The Genesis of Islam in Malabar,' *Indica* 6, 1 (March 1969): 1-13.

Cherian, Thomas, 'West Asian Contribution to the Malayalam

Language and Culture of Kerala and Kerala Christians.' www.geocities.com/pec19man/Malayalam.doc

Dasgupta, Ashin, *Malabar in Asian Trade, 1740-1800* (London: Cambridge University Press, Cambridge South Asian Studies, 1967).

Dasgupta, Ashin, and M.N. Pearsons, eds., *India and the Indian Ocean 1500-1800* (Calcutta: Oxford University Press, 1987).

Duvigneau, A.B., 'Saint Thomas: A-t-il Porté l'Évangile jusqu'en Chine?,' *Bulletin Catholique de Pekin* (January-October 1936): 18-37.

Firth, Cyril Bruce, *An Introduction to Indian Church History* (Madras: Christian Literature Society, 1961).

Flusser, David, 'The People of the (prayer)book,' *Jerusalem Post International Edition* (20 June 1992): 10.

Friedmann, Y., 'Qissat Shakarwatî Farmâd: A Tradition Concerning the Introduction of Islam to Malabar,' *Israel Oriental Studies* 5 (1975): 233-45.

Galletti, A., A.J. Van Der Burg and P. Groot, *The Dutch in Malabar: Selections from the Records of the Madras Government* (Madras: Government Press, 1911).

Gantzer, Hugh and Colleen, 'Pepper: The Little Master,' *New India Digest* 57 (1997): 24-6.

Hosten, Rev. J., *The Song of Thomas Ramban* (Cochin: Union Press, 1930).

Hunt, W.S., *The Anglican Church in Travancore and Cochin, 1816-1916* (Kottayam: Church Missionary Society Press, 1968).

Iyer, K.V. Krishna, 'Kerala's Relations with the Outside World,' in S.S. Koder et al., eds., *Commemoration Volume* (Cochin: The Kerala History Association and The Cochin Synagogue Quatercentenary Celebration Committee, 1971): 65-77.

Iyer, L.K. Anantha Krishna, *The Cochin Tribes and Castes*, 2 vols. (Madras: Government of Cochin; and London: Luzac & Co., 1909 & 1912).

Iyer, V.R. Krishna, 'Cultural Autonomy,' in S.S. Koder et al., eds., *Commemoration Volume* (Cochin: The Kerala History

Association and The Cochin Synagogue Quatercentenary Celebration Committee, 1971): 277-87.

Joseph, T.K., 'Review of Fr. I. Daniel's *The Syrian Church of Malabar*,' *Journal of Indian History* 26, 3 (*c*. 1946): 301-19.

Khan, Mohibul Hassan, 'Unity in Diversity,' in S.S. Koder et al., eds., *Commemoration Volume* (Cochin: The Kerala History Association and The Cochin Synagogue Quatercentenary Celebration Committee, 1971): 139-42.

Kleeblatt, Norman L., and Vivian B. Mann, *Treasures of the Jewish Museum* (New York: Universe, 1986).

Kohut, George Alexander, 'Les Juifs dans les colonies Hollandaises,' *Revue des Études Juives* 31 (n.d.): 293-7.

Kusuman, K.K., *A History of Trade and Commerce in Travancore (1600-1805)* (Delhi: Mittal Publications, 1987).

Lawson, C.A., *British and Native Cochin* (Cochin: Courier Press, 1860).

Lininer, Elias, *Gaspar da Gama: Um Converso de Cabral* (Rio de Janeiro, Editora Nova Fronteira, 1987, *c*.1986). [In Portuguese.]

Logan, William, *Malabar*, vol. 1 (Trivandrum: Charithram Publications, 1981).

Mathew, P.V., *Acta Indica: The Acts of St. Thomas in India* (Ernakulam: The Author, 1986).

Menon, A. Sreedhara, *Social and Cultural History of Kerala* (New Delhi: Sterling Publishers, 1984a).

———, *A Survey of Kerala History* (Madras: S. Viswanathan, 1984b).

Menon, C. Achyuta, *The Cochin State Manual* (Ernakulam: Cochin Government Press, 1911).

Miller, Peter, 'Kerala: Jewel of India's Malabar Coast,' *National Geographic* 173, 5 (May 1988): 592-617. [Photographs by Raghubir Singh.]

Moens, The Rt. Worshipful Adriaan, *Memorandum on the Administration of the Coast of Malabar, Dated 18th April 1781 A.D.*, trans. Rev. P. Groot and A. Galletti, notes by A. Galletti (New Delhi: Usha Publications, rpt. 1984).

Narayanan, M.G.S., *Cultural Symbiosis in Kerala* (Trivandrum: Kerala Historical Society, 1972).

Pillai, Elankulam Kunjan, *Studies in Kerala History* (Trivandrum: 1970).

Pisharoti, K.R., 'Cranganur: A Study,' *Bulletin of the Rama Varma Research Institute* (1930): 33-6.

Rao, T.A.G., 'Three Inscriptions of Sthanu Ravi,' *Travancore Archæological Series* 2 (1920): 60-86.

Spear, Percival, *India: A Modern History* (Ann Arbor: University of Michigan Press, 1961): 73.

Subrahmanyam, Sanjay, *The Political Economy of Commerce: Southern India, 1500-1650* (Cambridge: Cambridge University Press, 1990).

Thankappan Nair, P., 'Where Peaceful Co-Existence was a Way of Life: Cranganore, Trade Emporium of the East,' *The Sunday Standard* (Madras, 9 March 1969).

Thomas, P.J., 'The South Indian Tradition of the Apostle Thomas,' *Journal of the Royal Asiatic Society of Great Britain and Ireland*, Centenary Supplement (October 1924): 213-23.

———, 'Roman Trade Centres in Malabar,' *Kerala Society Papers* 2, 10 (1932): 259-70.

Thurston, Edgar, assisted by K. Rangachari, *Castes and Tribes of Southern India*, vol. II (Madras: Government Press, 1909).

Vellian, Jakob, 'The Jewish Christian Community of India,' *Judaism* 20, 1 (1971): 104-7.

Venn, T.W., *Cochin-Malabar: Palms and Pageants* (Calicut: Privately published, 1951).

Visscher, J.C., *Letters from Malabar* (Madras, 1862).

Whiteway, R.S., *The Rise of Portuguese Power in India, 1497-1550* (New York: Augustus M. Kelley Publishers, 1967 [1899]).

SCHOLARLY STUDIES OF THE COCHIN JEWS

There have been a surprising number of scholarly studies of the Cochin Jews. The best surveys of the history of the community are by Johnson (1975, 1982, 1986) and Katz and Goldberg (1989a, 1990, 1993b). Other important contributions are by Van Dort (1846), Raffalovich (1895), Slousch (1910), Reissner (1949) and Rabinowitz (1958). Weil (1982, 1986) studied Jewish-Christian relations in Kerala.

Ancient history, especially epigraphy and archaeology, was studied by Gundert (1844), Burnell (1874), Hultzsch (1894/5), Daniel (two articles of 1924), the eminent Indologist, S. Lévi (1926, 1930), Joseph (1929, 1930), Achan (1930, 1946), and Burkitt (1930). Many of the controversies raised in these articles were settled by Narayanan (1971).

One aspect of the Cochin community's history that has received a great deal of scholarly attention has been its infamous system of social organization. This 'Jewish apartheid' was the subject of articles by s'Gravezande (1778), DeCosta (1895), Marx (1930), Kloetzel (1938), Smythe and Gershuny (1956), Bar-Giora (1957), Segal (1967, 1983), Mendelbaum (1975) and Katz and Goldberg (1992).

The unique religious observances of Cochin were studied by Mendelbaum (1939, 1973) and Katz and Goldberg (two articles in 1989, one in 1990, books 1993 and 2005). Cochin weddings were observed and reported by Macfarlane (1937), Rabinowitz (1952), Caspi (1981) and Walerstein (1982, 1986). Cochin Hebrew liturgical music has been the domain of Spector (1969, 1971, 1972, 1985/6), although Ross (1977/8) has also contributed to this area. The Malayalam folk songs of the Cochin Jewish women were studied by Johnson (1979), Jussay (1978, 1982, 1984, 1986) and Isenberg, Daniel and Dekel-Squires (1984). Synagogues and synagogal life was the subject of an outstanding paper by Bar-Giora (1958, 1984), and Cochin Jewish literature was briefly surveyed by Fischel (1970/1, 1972). Greenbaum (1966, 1970) recorded keen observations made during his visit.

The reasons for the decline of the community was the subject of F. Hallegua's M.A. thesis (1984). Weil's 1984 edited book in

Hebrew contains many valuable studies, most of which dealing with the resettlement of Cochin Jews in Israel. Kushner (1968, 1976) provided a definitive, if somewhat dated, study of their adaptation to life in Israel. Other studies of this topic are by Guggenheim and Dreyfuss (1959), Mendelbaum (1981, 1986), Moscowtiz (1981) and Johnson (1985).

Achan, P. Anujan, 'A Hebrew Inscription from Chennamangalam,' *Indian Antiquary* 59 (1930): 134-5.

———, 'Trial Excavations at Cranganur,' *Bulletin of the Rama Varma Research Institute* 13 (July 1946): 40-2.

Amar, Ariella, and Ruth Jacoby, *V'kibatstim meyarketel-arets [Ingathering of the Nations. Treasures of Jewish Art: Documenting an Endangered Legacy]*, Eng. trans. by Andrew Lang and Michel Oren (Jerusalem: Center for Jewish Art, Hebrew University of Jerusalem, 1998): 106-15. See especially the chapter 'India'.

Bar-Giora, Naphtali, 'Sources-Materials for the History of the Relations between the White Jews and the Black Jews of Cochin,' *Sefunoth* 1 (1957): 242-78. [In Hebrew.]

———, 'A Note on the History of the Synagogues in Cochin,' *Sefunoth* 2 (1958): 214-45. [In Hebrew.]

———, 'Toldoth Beth-Hakeneseth b'Kogin,' in S. Weil, ed., *MiKotsin l'Eretz Yisroel* (Jerusalem: Kumu Brinah, 1984): 40-59. [In Hebrew.]

Bar-Ilan, Meir, 'The Discovery of *The Words of Gad the Seer*,' *Journal for the Study of the Pseudepigrapha* 11 (1993): 95-107.

Birnbaum, Ervin, 'David Reubeni's Indian Origin,' *Historia Judaica* 20, 1 (April 1958): 3-30.

Burkitt, F.C., 'Hebrew Signatures on the Copper-Plate,' *Kerala Society Papers* 6 (1930): 323.

Burnell, A.C., 'The Original Settlement-Deed of the Jewish Colony at Cochin,' *The Indian Antiquary* 3 (November 1874): 333-4.

Caspi, Mishael Maswari, 'Wedding Customs of the Jews of Cochin According to the Book of Poems and the Songs of Praise,' in Mishael Maswari Caspi, ed., *Jewish Tradition in the Diaspora:*

Studies in Memory of Walter J. Fischel (Berkeley, CA: Judah L. Magnes Museum, 1981): 231-8

Chakravarti, Ranabir, 'Review of N. Katz, *Who Are the Jews of India?* (2000),' *Journal of Indo-Judaic Studies* (Saskatoon) 4 (2001): 122-6.

Chiriyankandath, James, 'Nationalism, Religion and Community: A.B. Salem and the Disappearance of Cochin Jewry.' Unpublished paper, read at Centre for South Asian Studies Seminar, Cambridge University, 21 February 2001.

Daniel, K.N., 'Kottayam Plate of Vira-Raghava Chakravarti,' *The Indian Antiquary* 53 (1924): 185-96, 219-29, 244-51.

———, 'The Anchuvannam and the Manigramam of the Kottayam Plates of Tanu Iravi or the Jews and Christians of Malabar,' *Indian Antiquary* 53 (1924): 257-61.

DeCosta, A., 'The "White" and "Black" Jews of Malabar,' *India Church Quarterly Review* (April 1895): 106-25.

Egorova, iuliia Ivanovna, 'Evrei Indii (Kochinskia obshchina),' *Vostok* (Russia) 1996, no. 6: 28-33. [India's Jews: The Cochin Community.] [In Russian.]

Ezekiel, Joseph, and Joseph Jacobs, 'Cochin,' *The Jewish Encyclopedia* IV (1901): 135-8.

Fischel, Walter J., 'Cochin and Some Prominent Jewish Personalities,' in A. Berger, et al., eds., *The Joshua Block Memorial Volume: Studies in Booklore and History* (New York: New York Public Library, 1960): 151-64.

———,'Cochin in Jewish History: Prolegomena to a History of the Jews in India,' *Proceedings of the American Academy for Jewish Research* 30 (1962): 37-59.

———, 'From Cochin (India) to New York,' in *Harry Austrynn Wolfson Jubilee Volume* (Jerusalem: American Academy for Jewish Research, 1965).

———,'The Exploration of Jewish Antiquities of Cochin on the Malabar Coast,' *Journal of the American Oriental Society* 87 (1967): 230-48.

———, 'The Rotenburg Family in Dutch Cochin of the Eighteenth Century,' *Studia Rosenthaliana* 1 (1967): 32-44.

———, 'The Literary Creativity of the Jews of Cochin on the Malabar Coast,' *Jewish Book Annual* 28 (1970-1): 25-31.

———, 'The Contribution of the Cochin Jews to South Indian and Jewish Civilization,' in S.S. Koder et al., ed., *Commemoration Volume* (Cochin: The Kerala History Association and The Cochin Synagogue Quatercentenary Celebration Committee, 1971): 15-63.

Friedman, Maurice S., 'Review of N. Katz and E. Goldberg, *The Last Jews of Cochin* (1993),' *Shofar: An Interdisciplinary Journal of Jewish Studies* 17, no. 3 (1999): 113-15.

Gaguin, Shemtob, *Hayye HaYehudim be Cochin* (London: 1956). [In Hebrew.]

Gokhale, B.G., 'Review of N. Katz and E. Goldberg, *The Last Jews of Cochin* (1993),' *Choice* 31, 1 (September 1993): 188.

Gold, Daniel, 'Review of N. Katz and E. Goldberg, *The Last Jews of Cochin* (1993),' *Association for Jewish Studies Review* 20/2 (1995): 473-4.

Greenbaum, Aaron, 'The Cochin Jewish Community: Impressions from a Mission to India, 1966,' *Midrashita: A Journal Devoted to Halacha, Jewish Thought & Education* (Spring 1970): 82-94.

———, *Report on India, visited February-March 1966* (Jerusalem: American Joint Distribution Committee, 1966).

Guggenheim, K. and F. Dreyfuss, 'Food Habits and Food Consumption of Jews from Cochin in Israel,' *American Journal of Clinical Nutrition* 7, 3 (1959): 519-25.

Gundert, Rev. H., 'Hebrew Version of the Jewish Sasanam with the Translation into English together with a Notice on an Ancient Malayalim Poem called "The Song or Legend of Payanur",' *Madras Journal of Literature and Science* 31 (1844): 11-17.

Hacco, Galia, 'The Ritual Cycle of Cochin Jewish Holidays: A Malabari Perspective,' in Shalva Weil, ed., *India's Jewish Heritage: Ritual, Art, & Life-Cycle* (Mumbai: Marg Publications, 2002): 69-77.

Hallegua, Fiona, 'The Jewish Community of Cochin: Its Twilight

Years' (M.A. thesis, University of Kerala, St. Theresa's College, Ernakulam, March 1984).

Hallegua, Samuel H., 'The Marriage Customs of the Jewish Community of Cochin,' in Shalva Weil, ed., *India's Jewish Heritage: Ritual, Art, & Life-Cycle* (Mumbai: Marg Publications, 2002): 61-7.

———, 'The Jews in Kerala: A Response,' in Bosco Puthur, ed., *St. Thomas Christians and Nambudiris, Jews and Sangam Literature* (Kochi: L.R.C. Publications, 2003): 138-41.

Harman, William, 'Review of N. Katz and E. Goldberg, *The Last Jews of Cochin* (1993),' *Journal of the American Academy of Religion* LXIV, 2 (1996): 435-7.

Hultzsch, E., 'Cochin Plates of Bhaskara Ravivarman,' *Epigraphia Indica* 3, 11 (1894-5): 66-9.

Isenberg, Shirley Berry, Rivkah Daniel, and Miriam Dekel-Squires, *Tishah Shire-Am Yehudim be Malayalam* (Jerusalem, 1984). [In Hebrew and Malayalam.]

Johnson, Barbara C., 'Shingli or Jewish Cranganore in the Traditions of the Cochin Jews of India, with an Appendix on the Cochin Jewish Chronicles' (M.A. thesis, Smith College, 1975).

———, 'Malayalam Jewish Women's Songs: Themes and Social Context of Performance,' a paper delivered at the Association for Jewish Studies, 11th Annual Conference, Boston, 1979.

———, 'Cranganore, Joseph Rabban and Cheraman Perumal: Reconsideration of an Origin Theme in Cochin Jewish Folklore,' *Pe'amim* 13 (1982): 71-83. [In Hebrew.]

———, ' "Our Community" in Two Worlds: The Cochin Paradesi Jews in India and Israel' (Ph.D. dissertation, University of Massachusetts, 1985).

———, 'The Emperor's Welcome: Reconsiderations of an Origin Theme in Cochin Jewish Folklore,' in Thomas A. Timberg, ed., *The Jews of India* (New Delhi: Vikas, 1986): 161-76.

———, 'Remarkable Women in the Narrative Repertoire of a Cochin Jewish Storyteller: Gender Education Through Folklore,' A paper read at the annual meeting of the Association for Jewish Studies, Boston, 19 December 1994.

———, 'Cochin Jews and Kaifeng Jews: Reflections on Caste, Surname, "Community" and Conversion,' *Pe'amim* (1994): 32-48. [In Hebrew.]

———, ' "For Any Good Occasion We Call Them": Community Parties and Cultural Continuity among the Cochin Paradesi Jews of Israel,' in Nathan Katz, ed., *Studies of Indian-Jewish Identity* (New Delhi: Manohar, 1995).

———, 'Cochin Jews and Kaifeng Jews: Reflections on Caste, Surname, "Community" and Conversion,' in Jonathan Goldstein, ed., *The Jews of China*, vol. 1, *Historical and Comparative Perspectives* (Armonk NY: M.E. Sharpe, 1999): 104-19.

———, 'Cochin Jews,' in Michael Terry, ed., *Reader's Guide to Judaism* (Chicago: Fitzroy Dearborn, 2000): 117-18.

———. ' "Till the Women Finish Singing": Historical Overview of Cochin Jewish Women's Malayalam Songs,' *Journal of Indo-Judaic Studies* (Saskatoon) 4 (2001): 7-22.

———, 'New Research, Discoveries and Paradigms: A Report on the Current Study of Kerala Jews.' Paper read at 'A View from the Margin: The State of the Art of Indo-Judaic Studies,' Oxford Centre for Hebrew and Jewish Studies, U.K., 2 July 2002.

———, *Jewish Women's Song from Kerala: Oh, Lovely Parrot!*, With Scaria Zacharia (Jerusalem: The Hebrew University, Anthology of Music Traditions in Israel, 18, 2004).

Joseph, T.K., 'A Hebrew Inscription from Parur,' *Kerala Society Papers*, ser. 3 (1930): 166-8.

———, 'The Date of Bhâskara Ravi Varman (A Rejoinder),' *The Indian Antiquary* (February 1929): 21-7.

Jussay, P.M., 'The Malayalam Folk Songs of the Cochin Jews and the Light They Throw on Their History.' Paper read at the 39th session of the India History Congress, Osmania University, Hyderabad, 1978.

———, 'The Song of Evarayi,' *Pe'amim* 13 (1982): 84-95. [In Hebrew.]

———, 'The Song of Evarayi,' in S. Weil, ed., *MiKotsin l'eretz*

Yisroel, (Jerusalem: Kumu Brinah, 1984): 13-10. [In Hebrew.]

———, 'The Song of Evarayi,' in Thomas A. Timberg, ed., *The Jews of India*, (New Delhi: Vikas, 1986): 145-60.

———, 'The Wedding Songs of the Cochin Jews and of the Knanite Christians of Kerala: A Study in Comparison,' in Jacob Vellian, ed., *Symposium on Knanites: Conducted in Connected with the Platinum Jubilee Celebrations of the Diocese of Kottayam, on 29th August 1986* (Kottayam: Jothi Book House, 1986).

———'The Jews in Kerala,' in Bosco Puthur, ed., *St. Thomas Christians and Nambudiris, Jews and Sanham Literature* (Kochi: L.R.C. Publications, 2003): 126-37.

Katz, Nathan, 'Understanding Religion in Diaspora: The Case of the Jews of Cochin,' *Religious Studies and Theology* 15, 1 (1996): 5-17.

———, 'The Judaisms of Kaifeng and Cochin: Parallels and Divergences,' in Jonathan Goldstein, ed., *The Jews of China*, vol. I, *Historical and Comparative Perspectives* (Armonk NY: M.E. Sharpe, 1999): 120-48.

———, 'The Judaisms of Kaifeng and Cochin: Parallel and Divergent Styles of Religious Acculturation,' in Roman Malek, ed., *From Kaifeng . . . to Shanghai: Jews in China* (Sankt Augustin, Germany: Monumenta Serica Monograph Series XLVI, 2000): 173-92.

———, 'The Historical Traditions of the Jews of Kochi,' *Studies in History* 21, 2 n.s. (2005): 127-47.

Katz, Nathan, and Ellen S. Goldberg, 'Asceticism and Caste in the Passover Observances of the Cochin Jews,' *Journal of the American Academy of Religion* LVII, 1 (Spring 1989a): 53-82.

———, 'Passover in Cochin,' *Southeast Council Association for Asian Studies Annals* 10 (1989b): 99-113.

———, 'Ritual Enactments of Indian-Jewish Identity Among the Cochin Jews.' Paper read at the annual meeting of the American Academy of Religion, New Orleans, LA, 19 Novenber 1990.

———, 'The Ritual Enactments of the Cochin Jews: The Powers of Purity and Nobility,' *Journal of Ritual Studies* 4, 2 (1990): 199-238.

———, 'Jewish "Apartheid" and a Jewish Gandhi,' *Jewish Social Studies* L, 3-4 (Summer-Fall 1988-93): 147-76.

———, "Jewish 'Apartheid" and a Jewish Gandhi,' *Ethnic Studies Reports* 10, 2 (July 1992): 18-35.

———, 'The Synagogues of South India,' *Arts of Asia* 23, 1 (January-February 1993): 131-4.

———, *The Last Jews of Cochin: Jewish Identity in Hindu India* (Columbia, SC: University of South Carolina Press, 1993b).

———, 'The Sephardi Diaspora in Cochin, India,' *Jewish Political Studies Review* 3, 3-4 (Fall 1993c): 97-140.

———, 'The Ritual Enactments of Indian-Jewish Identity of the Cochin Jews,' in Nathan Katz, ed., *Studies of Indian-Jewish Identity* (New Delhi: Manohar, 1995).

———, 'Leaving Mother India: Reasons for the Cochin Jews' Leaving India,' *Population Review*, 39, 1 & 2 (1995): 35-53.

———, *Kashrut, Caste and Kabbalah: The Religious Life of the Jews of Cochin* (New Delhi: Manohar, 2005).

Kloetzel, C.Z., 'Anjuvanam Reise zu den Schwartzen und Weißen Juden in Cochin,' *Jüdische Revue, Sonderheft Judaica* (Mukacevo, C.S.R.: Nekuda Verlag, 1938). [In German.]

Kohut, George Alexander, 'Correspondence between the Jews of Malabar and New York a Century Ago,' in George Alexander Kohut, ed., *Semitic Studies in Memory of Rev. Dr. Alexander Kohut* (Berlin: S. Calvary & Co., 1897): 420-34.

Konner, Melvin, *Unsettled: An Anthropology of the Jews* (New York, Viking Compass, 2003): 208-14. [Chapter 10, 'Ends of the Earth: How Jews Thrived in Exotic Places,' a focus on the Cochin Jews.]

Kushner, Gilbert, 'Indians in Israel: Guided Change in a New-Immigrant Village,' *Human Organization* 27, 4 (1968): 352-61.

———, *Immigrants from India in Israel: Planned Change in an Administered Community* (Tucson: University of Arizona Press, 1973).

Leasure, J. William, 'Review of N. Katz and E. Goldberg, *The Last Jews of Cochin* (1993),' *Population Review* 39, 1 & 2 (1995): 120-2.

Lesley, Arthur M., 'Shingly Jews, the Pepper Trade, and Abarvanel's Redemption: Two New Documents from 1504.' A talk in the Library of Congress Hebraica Research Seminar, 1998.

———, 'Contrasting Reactions of Isaac Abravanel and Yohanan Alemanno to Reports of Jews in India,' Paper Read at the Renaissance Society of America Annual Conference (26 March 1999).

———, 'Shingly in Cochin Jewish Memory and in Eyewitness Accounts,' *Journal of Indo-Judaic Studies* (Saskatoon) 3 (2000): 7-20.

Lévi, Sylvan, 'Problemes Indo-Hébraïques,' *Revue des Études Juivres* 82 (1926): 45-54.

———, 'Quelques documents nouveaux sur les Juifs du sud de l'Inde,' *Revue des Études Juivres* 89 (1930): 26-32.

Lord. Rev. J. Henry, 'Jews in Cochin,' in J. Hastings, ed., *Encyclopaedia of Religion and Ethics* (London, 1960), 7: 557-9.

Macfarlane, Eileen W.E., 'The Racial Affinities of the Jews of Cochin,' *Journal of the Royal Asiatic Society of Bengal* 3 (1937): 1-23.

———, 'A White Jew's Wedding,' *Maharaja's College Magazine* 19 (1937): 1-7.

Malekandanthil, Pius, 'The Jews of Cochin and the Portuguese: 1498-1663,' *Proceedings of the Indian History Congress* (62nd Session, Bhopal, 2001), (Kolakata: Indian History Congress, 2002): 239-55.

Mandelbaum, David G., 'The Jewish Way of Life in Cochin,' *Jewish Social Studies* 1, 4 (October 1939): 423-60.

———, 'The Sukkot Observance in Cochin,' in Philip Goodman, ed., *The Sukkot and Simhat Torah Anthology* (Philadelphia: Jewish Publication Society, 1973): 231-3.

———, 'Social Stratification Among the Jews of Cochin in India and in Israel,' *The Jewish Journal of Sociology* 17, 2 (1975): 165-210.

———, 'A Case History of Judaism: The Jews of Cochin in India and in Israel,' in Misael Maswari Caspi, ed., *Jewish Tradition in the Diaspora: Studies in Memory of Walter J. Fischel* (Berkeley, CA: Judah L. Magnes Museum, 1981): 211-30.

———, 'Social Stratification among the Jews of Cochin in India and in Israel,' in Thomas A. Timberg, ed., *Jews in India* (New Delhi: Vikas, 1986): 61-120.

Marx, Alexander, 'Contributions a l'Histoire des Juifs de Cochin,' *Revue des Études Juives* 89 (1930): 293-304.

Moscowitz, Stuart B., 'Transfer of Religious Symbols of Ethnic Identity from India to Israel: Cochini Identity.' Paper Read at the Israel Anthropological Society Annual Convention, Haifa, February 1981.

———, 'The Cochini Transformed: Emerging Ethnic Identity among South India Jews in Israel.' Ph.D. dissertation, Catholic University of America, 1986.

Mundadan, A. Mathian, CMI, 'The Jews in Kerala: A Response,' in Bosco Puthur, ed., *St. Thomas Christians and Nambudiris, Jews and Sanham Literature* (Kochi: L.R.C. Publications, 2003): 142-50.

Nandy, Ashis, 'Time Travel to a Possible Self: Searching for the Alternative Comopolitanism of Cochin', *Japanese Journal of Political Science* [Cambridge University Press] 1, no. 2 (November 2000): 295-327; 312-21. See especially 'The Jewish Diaspora'.

Narayanan, M.G.S., 'The Jewish Copper Plates of Cochin,' *Charitram Quarterly Journal* 3 (July-September 1971): 22-32.

———, 'Further Studies in The Jewish Copper Plates of Cochin.' Paper read at 'A View from the Margin: The State of the Art of Indo-Judaic Studies,' Oxford Centre for Hebrew and Jewish Studies, U.K., 2-6 July 2002.

———, 'Further Studies in The Jewish Copper Plates of Cochin,' *Journal of Indo-Judaic Studies* (Saskatoon) 6 (2003): 19-28.

Puthur, Bosco, ed., *St. Thomas Christians and Nambudiris, Jews and Sanham Literature* (Kochi: L.R.C. Publications, 2003).

Qafah, Yosef, 'Sror miktabim ben manhige yhude Cochin e'ben yhude teman ubabel (A Bundle of Letters Sent between the Leaders of the Jews of Cochin and the Jews of Yemen and Babylonia),' *Sinai* 19 (1972): 63-81. [In Hebrew.]

———, 'Od hamesh miktabim (Five Additional Letters),' *Sinai* 71 (1974): 62-71. [In Hebrew.]

Rabinowitz, Louis, 'A Jewish Wedding in South India,' *Jewish Affairs* (July 1952): 41-4.

———, 'A Note on the Origin of the Jews of Cochin,' *Jewish Quarterly Review* 47 (April 1958): 376-9.

Raffalovich, Samuel, *Kadmoniyoth Hayehoodim B'Malabar* (Antiquities of the Jews of Malabar), (Jerusalem: A.M. Lunoz, 1895) (also Ernakulam: Indo-Israel Publications, 1966). [In Hebrew.]

Rajasekaran, Vengal Chakkarai, 'Indian Jewry through the Ages,' *The Hindu* (2 June 1996): 27, col. a. [Review of N. Katz, ed., *Studies of Indian Jewish Identity* (1995).]

Reissner, H.G., 'The History of Cochin's Jewish Community,' *India and Israel* 2 (1949): 19-20.

———, 'Jews in Medieval Ceylon,' *Eastern World* 5 (1951): 14-16.

———, 'Jews in Medieval Ceylon,' *India and Israel* 9 (1951): 22-5.

———, 'Jews in Medieval Ceylon,' *The Ceylon Historical Journal* 3 (1953-4).

———, 'Benjamin of Tudela on Ceylon,' *The Ceylon Historical Journal* 3, 3/4 (1953-4): 228-33.

———, 'Benjamin of Tudela on Ceylon,' *Zeitschrift für Religions- und Geitesgeschichte* 6 (1954): 151-4.

Roland, Joan G., 'Review of R. Daniel and B. Johnson, *Ruby of Cochin* (1995),' *Points East* 12, 2 (July 1997): 19-20. [Hebrew version in *Pe'amim* (1997).]

———, 'Review of J.B. Segal, *A History of the Jews of Cochin* (1993),' *Journal of Indo-Judaic Studies* (Saskatoon) 1, 1 (1998): 107-10.

Ross, Israel J., 'Cultural Stability and Change in a Minority Group: A Study of the Liturgical and Folk Music of the Jews of Cochin, India.' D.S.M. thesis, Jewish Theological Seminary of America, 1977.

———, 'Cross-Cultural Dynamics in Musical Traditions: The Music of the Jews of Cochin,' *Musica Judaica* 2, 1 (5738/1977-8): 51-72.

Sabararatnam, Lakshmanan, 'Review of N. Katz and E. Goldberg, *The Last Jews of Cochin* (1993),' *Jewish Folklore and Ethnology Review* 15, 2 (1993): 158-9.

Sandberg, Dalia, 'A Cochini on an Israeli Moshav, What's in a Name?' M.A. thesis, Adelphi University, 1987.

Segal, J.B., 'The Jews of Cochin and Their Neighbours,' in H.J. Zimmels, J. Rabbinowitz and I. Finestein, eds., *Essays Presented to Chief Rabbi Israel Brodie on the Occasion of his Seventieth Birthday* (London: Soncino Press, Jews' College Publications n.s., no. 3, 1967).

———, 'White and Black Jews at Cochin: The Story of a Controversy,' *Journal of the Royal Asiatic Society* 2 (1983): 228.

———, *A History of the Jews of Cochin* (London: Valentine Mitchell, 1993).

———, 'The Jewish Community of Cochin, South India,' in Sidney L. Shipton, ed., *Unity in Diversity: Ta'ali World Movement for a United Israel* (Cheshire: Hochland & Hochland, 1996): 38-47.

Sinclair-Brull, Wendy, 'Not So Black and White: The Jews of Cochin, South India,' *Australian Journal of Jewish Studies* 5, 1 (1991): 93-109.

s'Gravezande, Adrianus, 'Geschiedkundige Narichten, Betreffende de Blanke en Swarte Jooden, te Cochim,' *Verhandelingen Door Het Genootschap der Wetenschapen te Vlissingen* (Middleburg) 6 (1778). [In Dutch.]

Shokeid, Moshe, 'Moshav Sela: Frustration and Crisis in the Process of Absorption,' in Ovadia Shapiro, ed., *Rural Settlements of New Immigrants in Israel: Development Problems of New Rural Communities* (Rehovot: Settlement Study Center, 1971): 103-23.

Slater, Matthew D., 'The Jews of Cochin,' *Judaism: A Quarterly Journal* 24, 4 (1975): 482-94.

Slousch, N., 'Les Juifs et le Judaïsme aux Indes,' *Révue du Monde Mussulman* 4 (1910): 726-69.

Smythe, H.H., and T. Gershuny, 'Jewish Castes of Cochin, India,' *Sociology and Social Research* 41, 2 (1956): 108-11.

Spector, Johanna, 'Jewish Songs from Cochin, India, with Special Reference to Cantillation and Shingly Tunes,' *Proceedings of the Fifth World Conference of Jewish Studies* (Jerusalem, 1969), IV: 245-65.

———, 'The Music of the Jews of Cochin with Special Reference to Shingli Tunes,' in S.S. Koder et al., eds., *Commemoration Volume* (Cochin: The Kerala History Association and The Cochin Synagogue Quatercentenary Celebration Committee, 1971): 177-85.

———, 'Shingli Tunes of the Cochin Jews,' *Asian Music* 3, 2 (1972): 23-8.

———, 'Yemenite and Babylonian Elements in the Musical Heritage of the Jews of Cochin, India,' *Musica Judaica: Journal of the American Society for Jewish Music* 7, 1 (5745/1985-6): 1-22.

Suri, Elizabeth, 'A Demographic Survey of the Cochin Jewish Community (Preliminary Report),' in E. Elias and E. Issac, eds., *Jews in India '64 with Who Is Who* (Ernakulam: Indo-Israel Publications, 1965): 35-9.

Tavim, José Alberto Rodrigues da Silva, *Judeus e Cristáos-Novos de Cochim História e Memória (1500-1662)* (Braga, Portugal: Edicóes Appacdm Distrial de Bragam 2003). [In Portuguese.]

Van Dort, Leopold Immanuel Jacob, 'The Jews in Cochin,' *The Jewish Chronicle* 3, 6 (December 1846): 167-70.

Walerstein, Marcia, 'The Cochini Jewish Wedding of the Malabar Community in India and Israel: Change in Custom, Symbol and Meaning,' in Issachar Ben-Ami, ed., *The Sephardi and Oriental Jewish Heritage* (Jerusalem: The Magnes Press, 1982): 529-50.

———, 'The Cochini Jewish Wedding of the Malabar Community in India and Israel: Change in Custom, Symbol and Meaning,' in Thomas A. Timberg, ed., *Jews in India* (New Delhi: Vikas, 1986): 248-70.

———, 'Public Rituals among the Jews of Cochin, India, in Israel:

Expressions of Ethnic Identity' (Ph.D. dissertation, UCLA, 1987).

Wasserstein, Asher, and Ya'akov El'azar, *Mi-minhage ha-Yerushalmiyim ha-Sefaradiyim. Mi-minhage Yahadut Kots'in* (Yerushalayim: Misrad ha-hinukh veha-tarbut, Agaf ha-hinukh ha-dati veha-Agaf le-shiluv moreshet Yahadut ha-Mizrah, 1988).

Weil, Ilana, 'The Architecture of the Paradesi Cochin Synagogue,' in Shalva Weil, ed., *India's Jewish Heritage: Ritual, Art, & Life-Cycle* (Mumbai: Marg Publications, 2002): 51-9.

Weil, Shalva, 'Symmetry between Christians and Jews in India: The Cnanite Christians and the Cochin Jews of Kerala,' *Contributions to Indian Sociology* 16, 2 (1982): 175-96.

———, ed., *From Cochin to the Land of Israel* (Jerusalem: Kumu Berina, 1984). [In Hebrew.]

———, 'Symmetry between Christians and Jews in India: The Cnanite Christians and the Cochin Jews of Kerala,' in Thomas A. Timberg, ed., *Jews in India* (New Delhi: Vikas, 1986): 177-204.

———, 'Cochin Jews,' in Paul Hockings, ed., *Encyclopedia of World Cultures*, vol III: *South Asia* (Boston: G.K. Hall & Co., 1992): 713.

———, 'Cochin Jews,' in Carol R. Ember, Melvin Ember, and Ian Skoggard, eds., *Encyclopedia of World Cultures Supplement* (New York: Macmillan Reference, 2002): 78-80.

Weinstein, Brian, 'Jewish Pepper Traders of the Malabar Coast: The Rahabis,' *Journal of Indo-Judaic Studies* 5 (Saskatoon) (June 2002): 40-54.

Weinstein, Myron M., 'A Putative Ceylon Rite,' in Charles Berlin, ed., *Studies in Jewish Bibliography, History and Literature in Honor of I. Edward Kiev* (New York: Ktav, 1971): 495-509.

———, 'A Hebrew Qur'an Manuscript,' in Thomas A. Timberg, ed., *Jews in India* (New Delhi: Vikas, 1986): 205-47.

Whitehouse, T., *Some Historical Notices of Cochin on the Malabar Coast* (Kottayam: C.M. Press, 1859).

Zacharia, Scaria, 'Possibilities of Understanding Jewish Malayalam

Folksongs.' Paper read at 'A View from the Margin: The State of the Art of Indo-Judaic Studies,' Oxford Centre for Hebrew and Jewish Studies, U.K., 2-6 July 2002.

———, 'Possibilities of Understanding Jewish Malayalam Folksongs,' *Journal of Indo-Judaic Studies* (Saskatoon) 6 (2003): 29-47.

Zacharia, Scaria and Ophra Gamliel, with an Afterword by Barbara C. Johnson, *Yofehfiyah – Shirot Hanashim shel Yehidu Kerala [Oh Lovely – Songs of the Women of the Kerala Jews]* (Jerusalem: Ben-Zvi Institute, 2000). [In Hebrew and Malayalam, with an Afterword in English.]

GENERAL & NEWSPAPER ACCOUNTS OF THE COCHIN JEWS

Included with general interest accounts are writings by members of the Cochin community, some of which are excellent and reliable. One ought to begin with the synagogue's 400th anniversary commemoration (Koder, ed. 1971) which contains papers on Kerala's religious and cultural heritage, studies of the Cochin Jews' history, literature and music, and testimonials from such dignitaries as the late Smt. Indira Gandhi.

The historical writings and translations by Koder (1951, two in 1965, 1973, 1986) are outstanding. Important contributions were also made by I.B.E. Hallegua (1895, 1906) and I.S. Hallegua (1988). Other important contributions by Cochin Jews are found in section II.A. Sheth (1987, 1988) published some excellent photographs, and novelist Pierre Loti (1902) and traveller Lowell Thomas (1930) also left significant descriptions.

Adoor, K.K., 'The Story of the Coming of the Jews to Kerala,' in E. Elias & E. Isaac, eds., *Jews in India '64 with Who Is Who* (Ernakulam: Indo-Israel Publications, 1965): 7-14.

Aiyar, C.V. Subrahmanya, 'The Jews of Cochin,' *Malabar Quarterly Review* 1, 2 (June 1902).

Anonymous, *Story of the Willow Pattern Tiles* (Cochin: n.d.).
———, 'Notices of the Jews of Cochin,' *Oriental Christian Spectator* 10, 9 (1839): 389-97.
———, ('A.W.'), 'Jews in Cochin and the Malabar Coast,' *Jewish Chronicle* (18 May 1906): 15.
———, 'Cochin Jewry is Losing its Struggle to Remain Visible,' *New York Times* (3 October 1974).
———, 'Jews Street Bereft of Jews,' *Indian Express* (12 July 1983).
———, 'Wedding in Four-century Old Synagogue After Eight Years,' *The Hindu* (19 June 1986).
———, 'Jewish Antiquities Taken Out of Country,' *Statesman* (20 October 1991).
———, 'Local Couple Authors Book on Demise of Jewish Community in Cochin, India,' *Jewish Press of Tampa/Pinellas* (19-20 March 1993): 3. [Review of N. Katz and E. Goldberg, *The Last Jews of Cochin* (1993)].
———, 'Jewish Community in Cochin Chronicled by Katz & Goldberg,' *India Times* (30 April 1993): 15. [Review of N. Katz and E. Goldberg, *The Last Jews of Cochin* (1993).]
———, 'The Last Jews of India,' *JUF News* (Chicago, May 1993): 27, 31. [Review of N. Katz and E. Goldberg, *The Last Jews of Cochin* (1993).]
———, 'Near Extinct Jewish Community Chronicled by USF Scholar,' *USF Magazine* 35, 3 (Summer 1993): 17. [About of N. Katz and E. Goldberg, *The Last Jews of Cochin* (1993).]
———, 'History of Near Extinct Jews of South India,' *News India-Times* (17 September 1993): 45. [About N. Katz and E. Goldberg, *The Last Jews of Cochin* (1993).]
———, 'Kerala Jews Facing Extinction,' *The Statesman* (8 February 1994).
———, 'Shabdai S. Koder, 86, Jewish Leader in India' (obituary), *New York Times* (17 March 1994): C18.
———, 'A Synagogue Makes Aliyah,' *Rhode Island Jewish Herald* (31 August 1995): 8.
———, 'Just as it's Like Back Home,' *Indian Express* (5 October

1996). [Photo of Israeli Ambassador's visit to Cochin Synagogue, by P.K. Jeevan Jose.]

———, 'Tales from Shiraz and Cochin,' *Life and Religion* 1 (U.K., 1996): 14-17.

———, 'Queen Elizabeth, Duke visit Kochi,' *The Hindu* (18 November 1997).

———, 'In Search of the Beloved,' *Asian Age* (11 January 1998): 1, 18. [Review of Achala Moulik, *Earth Is But a Star*.]

———, 'Ghosts of the Spice Trade,' *IsraelWire 'Focus'* (30 March 1999) http://www.israelwiredaily@vjlists.com

———, 'Explore Jewish History in the Towns of India,' *Suburban Town News* (Paramus NJ, 7 April 1999): 75-6.

———, 'Repairs and Planning: Cochin Synagogue [Cochin, India],' *Kol India* IX, 1 (Mumbai, September 1999): 7, 24.

———, 'In Kochi, 15 Jews waited for Sharon,' *rediff.com* (8 September 2003) http://www.rediff.com/news.2003/sep/08sharon4/htm

———, 'Leave the Lamps Burning: History by the Numbers,' *Hadassah Magazine* (January 2005): 72.

———, 'Jewish Body to Honour Cochin Royal Family,' *newindpress.com* (15 February 2005). swww.newindpress.com/Print.asp?ID-IE20050213113642

———, 'Historic Visit of Jewish Delegation to Tripunithura Kalikotta Palace,' *Points East* 20/2 (Palo Alto, CA, July 2005): 12.

Barmouth, Eliahu, *In Search of Roots: The History and Folklore of the Cochin Jews* (Jerusalem: Privately published 2001). [56 pages in Hebrew, 20 pages in English.]

Basu, Nupur, 'Cochin Heritage To Be Preserved,' *India Abroad* (1 November 1991): 8.

Benjamin, J.M., ed., *Jews of Cochin, India* (New Delhi: Jewish Welfare Assn., 1999).

Berkson, Carmel, 'The Synagogue: The Jewish Heritage,' from *Splendours of Kerala* (Bombay: Marg Publications, 1979) [rept. 1983]): 116-18.

Bernstein, Elizabeth, 'The Jewish Traveler: Cochin,' *Hadassah Magazine* (February 1995): 30-3.

Bhatia, Arun, 'Down Jew Lane,' *Deccan Herald* (22 October 1995): 5.

———, 'Fading Glory,' *Times of India* (28 January 2000): 7.

Birnbaum, Solomon, 'India Through Jewish Eyes: A Pre-teen Travels to the Subcontinent,' *Jewish World* (New York, 28 January-3 February 2005): 11, 32.

Brenner, Frederic, *Les juifs de l'Inde: exposition de photographies de Frederic Brenner du 12 mai au 30 juin 1985* (Paris: Musee d'art juif de Paris, 1985).

Busi, Giulio, 'Una Sinagoga accanto a Shiva,' *Il Sole 24 Ore* (Italy) (14 January 2001): 39. [In Italian.]

Chhaya, Mayank, 'The Jewish Community of Cochin,' *India Abroad* (10 January 1992): 18.

Daniel, Ruby (Rivkah), 'Cochin's Kadavumbaham [*sic*] Synagogue,' *Points East* 8, 1 (February 1993): 5-6.

———, 'More Memories of Cochin's Jew Town,' *Bridges* 7, 1 (1997/8): 39-42.

Dawkins, Jim, 'The Last Jews of Cochin,' *Jewish Press of Pinellas County* 2, 4 (18 September 1987).

———, 'The Last Jews of Cochin: A USF Professor and his Wife Chronicle the Remaining Days of a Centuries-Old Community in India,' *USF Close Up Magazine* 30, 1 (Spring 1988): 4C-5C. [Photographs by Ellen S. Goldberg.]

Elijah, Samuel H., 'Cochin, India Synagogue,' *Philatelic Judaica Journal* 17, 4 (December 1968): 539-46.

———, 'An Interesting Cover from the State of Cochin,' *Judaica Post : Journal of Philatelic Judaica* (n.d.): 117-18.

Ezekiel, Gul-Fraaz N., 'Jew Town on Celluloid,' *Indian Express Weekend* (15 June 1991). [Review of Chetan Shah's film.]

———, 'A Disappearing Community,' *Jerusalem Post* (17 September 1991).

Faig, Ron, 'Near Extinct Jewish Community is Chronicled by Scholar,' *The Covenant* (Toronto, April 1993): 12. [About N.

Katz and E. Goldberg, *The Last Jews of Cochin* (1993).]

Fernandez, Maxwell, 'Jews of Kerala: End of the Road,' *The Week* (6-12 February 1983): 31-5.

Filkins, Dexter, 'Jewish Community in Coastal Town is Mere Shadow of Old Self,' *Los Angeles Times* (16 March 2000). Reprinted: 'Jewish Enclave in India is Down to Its Last Few,' *Philadelphia Inquirer* (16 April 2000): A22. Reprinted: 'Indian Twilight,' *Jerusalem Post* (21 April 2000): B6.

Foulds, Russel J., 'How Jewish was my Cochin,' *Sunday Times of India* (31 May 1992).

Fuks, Suzon, *Keeping the Light: A Diary of South India* (no publication data; privately published, *c.* 1997).

Geller, Doron, 'On Sacred Ground: Going Back to Jericho,' *Jewish Press* (Brooklyn, 29 December 2000): 118. [Discusses similarity of ancient Jericho synagogue inscriptions with Cochin prayer books.]

George, O.J., 'Diminishing Jewish Community of Cochin,' *Indian Express* (13 April 1987).

Gezari, Janet, 'A Synagogue in India: Discovering an Island of Tolerance,' *Connecticut College Magazine* (Fall 2001): 18-19.

Golan, Patricia, 'The Jews of India in Israel,' *News from Israel* (May 1990): 14.

Goldberg, Ellen S. and Nathan Katz, 'After 2,000 years in India, a Jewish Community Nears Extinction,' *Christian Science Monitor* (13 October 1984).

Goodman, Matthew, 'The Food Maven: Geography of Flavor Tackles Taste From Cochin to Yemen,' *Forward* (New York, 6 June 2003): 13-14.

Gopalakrishnan, C.V., 'Shedding an Aloofness,' *The Hindu* (26 Janunary 1997). [About N. Katz and E. Goldberg, *The Last Jews of Cochin* (1993).]

Gorenberg, Gershom, 'A Successful Transplant,' *Hadassah Magazine* (January 1990): 18-21.

Greenberg, Richard, 'Subcontinent Sojourn: Glimpsing a Jewish

"Brigadoon",' *B'nai B'rith Magazine* (Washington, Winter 2003).

Hallegua, Isaac Ben Elias, 'Letter of 1895 to Rev. J.H. Lord, Bombay,' Sassoon mss. 935.

——— (Anonymous), 'Malabar Jews I and II,' *Jewish Chronicle* (5 October 1906): 20-1; (19 October 1906): 31.

Hallegua, I.S., *The Paradesi Synagogue of Cochin and Its Dying Community of Jews* (Cochin: Manuscript, 1988).

Hallegua, S.H., 'Simchat Torah in Cochin,' *Kol Bina* 6, 1 (September 1986): 6.

Hansen, Barbara, 'Symbols May Surprise Visitors to Synagogue,' *Los Angeles Times* (24 September 1989): 10-11.

———, 'India's Jews Keep the Lamp Burning in Cochin,' *Newsday* (22 October 1989): 17.

———, 'A Synagogue in India among Hindu Shrines,' *Philadelphia Inquirer* (October 1989).

———, 'Synagogue Stands out as Unusual Tourist Landmark in Mostly Hindu India,' *The Star-Ledger* (22 October 1989): 11.

Horowitz, Martin, 'A Visit to Cochin,' *Jewish Affairs* 42, 2 (February 1987): 26-32.

Irani, Gustasp, 'Indian Sunset,' *Inside* (Fall 1993): 56-60.

Isaacs, Laurence, 'Journey to Jewish India,' *Reform Judaism* (Fall 1991): 36-7.

Jackson, Livia Bitton, 'The Women of Cochin,' *Jewish Press* (Brooklyn, 9 May 2003): M3.

Jacob, P., 'The Jews of Cochin,' *Frontline* (8-22 January 1988): 70-6.

James, Bonnie, 'Israeli Jews come in Search of Their Roots,' *Indian Express* (Trivandrum, 16 December 1995.

John, Binoo K., 'The Synagogue That Survived,' *Indian Express* (5 September 1999): 4.

Johnson, Barbara C., 'Jacob E. Cohen: In Memoriam (1913-1999),' *Journal of Indo-Judaic Studies* (Saskatoon) 3 (2000): 144-5.

———, 'Ruby Daniel: In Memoriam, 1917-2002,' *Journal of Indo-Judaic Studies* (Saskatoon) 6 (2003): 110-12.

Jose, Girija, 'Jews of Kochi: Exodus to Fatherland,' *Aside* (15 May 1994): 24-7.

Jose, P., 'End of a Great Tradition: Zion Beckons Cochin Jews,' *Sunday* (25 September 1983): 6-7.

Joshi, Pratik, 'Framing the Essence,' *Pioneer* (16 June 1993). [Review of Arun Chandha's film about Cochin Jews.]

Kamenetz, Rodger, 'Assimilation on the Sub-Continent: India's Jews Present a Study in Adaptation to Local Mores,' *The Forward* (New York, 11 June 1993): 9-10. [Review of N. Katz and E. Goldberg, *The Last Jews of Cochin* (1993).]

Kann, Peter, 'Lure of Israel Leads to the Demise of a 2,000-Year-Old Colony in India,' *The National Observer* (5 October 1970).

Kanter, R.J., 'Cochin and the Jews: An Indian Adventure,' *Kadimah* (Summer 2005): 3-4.

Kasriel, Emily, 'The Last Jews of Cochin, India,' *Brooklyn Jewish Press* (4 April 1997): 39. [Reprinted from *Jerusalem Post*; also on *The Jerusalem Post Internet Page* judaica.htm#events (25 March 1997).]

Katz, Nathan, 'On the Other Side: The Absence of anti-Jewish Sentiment is a Matter of Pride for both Jews and Gentiles in India,' *Dimensions* (Winter 1997): 91-2.

Katz, Nathan and Ellen S. Goldberg, 'The Jews of Cochin: Why Are They Leaving India?,' *St. Petersburg Times* (23 November 1985).

———, 'The Jews of Cochin: Living in Past Glory,' *Boston Jewish Advocate* (13 March 1986).

———, 'The Jews of Cochin,' *Midstream: A Monthly Jewish Review* 34, 2 (February/March 1988): 41-4.

Kaufman, Michael T., 'In Malabar, a Vivid Tapestry of the World's Faiths,' *New York Times* (19 December 1980).

Khan, Geoffrey, 'Ben Segal: Public-spirited Scholar of Aramaic and Hebrew Studies,' *The Guardian* (Manchester, England, 9 December 2003).

Kimor, Emma, 'A Visit to the Cochin Synagogue,' in Karen Primack, ed., *Under One Canopy: Readings in Jewish Diversity* (Silver Spring MD, Kulanu, 2003): 122-4.

Kin, Lai Kwok, 'A Few of Cochin's Jews Are Staying On,' *India Abroad* (16 October 1987): 43.

Koder, S.S., 'The Jews of Malabar,' *India and Israel* (1951): 31-5.

———, 'Kerala and Her Jews.' Paper read before the Kerala History Convention, 18 May 1965, privately published in Cochin, n.d.

———, 'Kerala and Her Jews,' in E. Elias & E. Isaac, eds., *Jews in India '64 with Who Is Who* (Ernakulam: Indo-Israel Publications, 1965): 21-34.

———, 'Hospitality and Tolerance,' in S.S. Koder et al., eds., *Commemoration Volume* (Cochin: The Kerala History Association and The Cochin Synagogue Quatercentenary Celebration Committee, 1971), pp. 1-4.

———, 'History of the Jews of Kerala,' *The St. Thomas Christian Encyclopaedia of India* 2 (1973): 183-5.

———, *History of the Jews of Kerala* (Cochin: Privately published, 1974).

———, 'Saga of the Jews of Cochin,' in Thomas A. Timberg, ed., *Jews in India* (New Delhi: Vikas, 1986): 121-42.

Koder, S.S., et al., eds., *Commemoration Volume: Cochin Synagogue Quartercentenary Celebrations* (Cochin: The Kerala History Association and The Cochin Synagogue Quatercentenary Celebration Committee, 1971).

Koder, S.S. and Fiona Hallegua, *Kerala and Her Jews* (no publication data, Cochin, *c*. 1995).

Kopf, Shula, 'Pearls of Ancient Wisdom,' *Jerusalem Post* (20 September 2002): 7-9.

Koya, C.H. Mohamed, 'A Unique Event in History,' in S.S. Koder et al., eds., *Commemoration Volume* (Cochin: The Kerala History Association and The Cochin Synagogue Quatercentenary Celebration Committee, 1971): 205-9.

Kresh, Paul, 'Trio of Jewish Films at Festival,' *New York Jewish Week* (25 September-1 October 1992): 43. [Includes review of J. Spector's film.]

Kress, W.H., 'Jews of Malabar,' *Asia* 36, 9 (1936).

Krishnanunny, K.P., 'Will Abraham's Flock Desert Its Synagogue?' *Indian Express* (*c*. 1983).

Krueger, Jerry, 'More on Indian Jewish Community,' *The Jewish State* (Highland Park, NJ, 9 April 1998): 4. [Letter-to-the-editor.]

Kutz, David, 'A Day in Cochin: A Visit to a 2,000-year-old Jewish Community in India,' *National Jewish Monthly* (April 1980): 6-7.

Lebenson, Beth I., 'Gaining a Jewish Identity: Through Buncher Leadership Program, young Jews are Revitalizing their Communities back Home,' *Philadelphia Jewish Exponent* (14 August 1997).

Lelyveld, Joseph, 'Mrs. Gandhi Wishes Jews "Mazel Tov",' *New York Times* (16 December 1968).

Leogrande, Dorine, 'Visitor from India: "We are All One," says Representative from Bombay,' *Hartford Jewish Ledger* (13 December 1996): 5.

Levenson, Gabe, 'Small Jewish Community adds Spice to Vivid Mix of Indian Society,' *Jewish Exponent* (Philadelphia, 28 February 1992): 4X-5X.

———, 'Passover in Jew Town,' *New York Jewish Week* (2-8 April 1993): 16, 42. [Review of N. Katz and E. Goldberg, *The Last Jews of Cochin* (1993).]

———, 'Celebrating New Year in Supersonic Jet Age: Customs may Vary but Message Remains the Same,' *Washington Jewish Week* (19 October 1995): 35.

———, 'Passage to India and Beyond,' *Jewish Week* (17 July 1998): 35.

Loti, Pierre, 'Chez les Maharajah du Travancore,' *Revue des Deux Mondes* 10 (1902): 241-95.

Macphedran, Gaby, 'Taste of the Indian South: Lovely Waterways, a Warm Welcome and Cochin's Jews are just a Few Reasons to visit Kerala,' *Jewish Chronicle* (17 November 1995): 43-5.

Manobla, Sara, 'The Cochin Connection,' *Jerusalem Post Magazine* (21 April 1989): 12-13.

Menon, Kesava, 'National Fervor Forced Jews to Migrate,' *The Hindu* (9 August 1995).

Menon, Leela, 'A Synagogue for a Song: An 800-year-old Synagogue in Kochi has been Ravaged and its Valuable Relics sent to Israel,' *Indian Express Sunday Magazine* (27 October 1991): 3.

Mohan, A.V.C., 'Cochin Jew Town: R.I.P.,' *Maharasthra Herald* (15 December 1995): 47.

Murphy, Paul, 'Cochin's Jews Prosper in Israel,' *India Abroad* (10 January 1992): 18.

Orbaum, 'What Israel was Meant to Be,' *Jerusalem Post* (4 October 1999): 6. [About Cochini immigrant, Nehemia Yitzhak.]

Parasarathy, Anand, 'Marriage of the Decade,' *Frontline* (9-22 January 1988): 77-9.

Passi, Sudha, 'Cochin Jews: Living on Borrowed Time,' *The Asian Age* (23 September 1996): 3.

Payyattil, Raj Gopal, 'Mixing with the Milieu,' *Indian Express*(Kochi) (30 November 2002): 4.

Pitchford, Ruth, 'Indian Jews Abandoning a Legacy of Two Millennia of Peace?,' *News India* (7 December 1990).

Poplak, R. Moshe Eliyahu, 'M a-Hodu v'ad . . . Cochin,' *Lamishpachah* (Adar 5758/ 1998): 6-7, 11. [In Hebrew.]

Prager, Jonas, 'The Last Generation,' *Jerusalem Post Magazine* (17 August 1984).

———, 'The Last Generation,' *Jerusalem Post International Edition* (19-24 August 1984): 12.

Primak, Karen, 'The Paradesi Synagogue Does Not Disappoint!,' *Kulanu* 11, no. 4 (Silver Spring, MD) (Winter 2004-5): 10.

Puthiakunnel, Thomas, 'Jewish Colonies of India Paved the Way for St. Thomas,' *The Malabar Church*, J. Vellan, ed., *Orientalia Christiana Analecta*, 186 (1970): 187-91.

Rae, George Milne, 'The Jews of Cochin,' *Madras Christian College Magazine* 6 (1888/9): 360-73.

Raghuraman, Geetha, 'The Diaspora fades away. . . ,' *The Hindu* (30 June 1997): IV, 1.

Raiff, Stan, 'Ancient Community Dispersing,' *Wurtsboro Jewish Star* (New York, July 1995): 19.

Raina, Divya, 'Films: Representing Things as They Are,' *Sunday Observer* (6-12 October 1991). [Review of Chetan Shah's film.]

Raju, R.K., 'The Jewish Tradition in India,' and 'Kerala Jews: A Vanishing Tribe,' *Mirror* (December 1988): 8-68.

Raskas, Bernard S., 'Jewish Indian Summer,' *Ohio Jewish Chronicle* (17 August 1995): 3.

Roby, N.E., 'The White Jews of Cochin,' *The Jewish Chronicle* (London, 6 September 1901): 17.

Rodin, Claudia, with photographs by Jason Lowe, 'The Last Jews of Cochin: On the Malabar Coast of India, a Small Jewish Community maintains Its Unique Customs and Cooking Styles,' *Food Illustrated* (June 1998): 62-9, 119.

Rosenhause, Sharon, 'India's Oldest Jewish Community Nears Extinction as Young Emigrate to Israel,' *Los Angeles Times* (9 January 1977).

Rosten, Leo, 'Cochin (India) Jews,' in *The Joys of Yiddish* (New York: Pocket Books, 1968): 472-3.

Rucker, Patricia, 'Cochin Jewry: A Community No More,' *Canadian Jewish News* (10 February 1994): 10.

Sabat, Upendra, 'Kerala Jews Need Funds to Fix Synagogues,' *News India-Times* (1 May 1998): 34.

Sahni, Julie, 'Passover in India: Why is this Night Different from all Others? Because we're Eating Coconut Rice,' *Los Angeles Times* (24 March 1991).

Sanghvi, Malavika, 'Such A Long Journey,' *Sunday Review* (14 August 1994): 8.

Saul, Karen, 'The Last Jew of Jews Street,' *Ha'aretz* (Jerusalem, 22 April 2003). [In Hebrew.]

Sengupta, Shivaji, 'On Keeping an Identity in India,' *India Abroad* (2 July 1993): 34. [Review of N. Katz and E. Goldberg, *The Last Jews of Cochin* (1993).]

Shankar, Lekha J., 'Kerala Calls: In Jerusalem's Israel Museum stands a Fond Tribute Recreated by the Jews who Left Kochi for the Promised Land,' *Hindustan Times* (18 April 1998): 7.

Sheth, Ketaki, 'The Jews of Cochin,' *The India Magazine* 7 (February 1987): 8-16.

———, 'Cochin's Jews: A Photo Essay,' *Present Tense* 15, 2 (January/February 1988): 32-5.

Sidhva, Shiraz, 'Rip-Off: A 16th-century Synagogue in Cochin is Stripped of its Artefacts for Export,' *Sunday* (4 November 1991).

Silver, Eric, 'Synagogue of the "Black Jews" : A 400-year-old Indian Structure Waits to be Rebuilt in Jerusalem,' *Jerusalem Report* (10 October 1991): 28-9.

———, 'Synagogue's Odyssey from Cochin Ends,' *Jewish Chronicle* (London, 11 October 1991).

———, 'Where the Maharajah Called: A Cochin Jew Recalls her Childhood "Synagogue of Miracles," now Restored in Jerusalem,' *Jerusalem Report* (13 July 1995): 34. [Reprint, 'A Cochin Jew Recalls Her Childhood "Synagogue of Miracles",' *Points East* 10, 3 (November 1995): 1, 5.]

———, '12th-century Ark Completes Israel Museum's Indian Synagogue,' *Jerusalem Report* (27 June 1996): 10.

Simon, A.I., 'The Rajahs of Cochin and the Jews,' *Maharaja's College Magazine* (Cochin) 23, 3 (n.d.).

Sofer, Tamar, 'India's Jews Lived Millennia without Anti-Semitism,' *Miami Jewish Tribune* (13-19 August 1993): 8A. [Review of N. Katz and E. Goldberg, *The Last Jews of Cochin* (1993).]

Soni, Charu, 'God's Lost Children,' *Sunday Mail* (6 October 1991).

Sreekala, S., 'The Indian Jewish Diaspora in Israel,' *Times of India* (17 October 1997): 7.

Thomas, Andoop, 'S. Koder: Patriarch of Jew Town,' *The Week* (1 April 1990): 37.

Thomas, Binu, 'The Last of the "White Jews",' *Jerusalem Post* (18 June 1991).

———, 'The Last of the "White Jews" of India,' *Points East* 8, 1 (February 1993): 9-10.

Thomas, Lowell, 'The City of Black and White Jews,' in *India: Land of the Black Pagoda* (New York and London: The Century Company, 1930): 28-39.

Trumbull, Robert, 'Malabar Jewish Colony's Return to Israel,' *The Times of India* (Bombay, 3 January 1954).

Varam, Dev, 'Jews of Kochi Waiting Eagerly for the Queen,' *Asian Age* (16 October 1997): 3.

———, 'Queen Elizabeth Visits Jewish Community,' *News India-Times* (24 October 1997): 48.

Wakabayashi, Gregory, 'Heat, Love, and Gods,' *Conde Nast Traveler* (June 1993): 99-163.

Wallach, Michael, 'Exotic Enclave of Indian Jews Legendary since Solomon,' *Canadian Jewish News* (4 August 1978).

Wariar, Shobha, 'The Vanishing Jews of Kochi,' *The Hindu* (31 March 1991).

Weintraub, Bernard, 'Jewish Community in India, Depleted by Emigration, Faces Dismal New Year,' *New York Times* (19 September 1974): L-9.

Weisman, Steven R., 'A Corner of India, Where a Minyan is Hard to Find,' *New York Times* (7 March 1986): A2.

———, 'Elegy for the Jews in a Corner of India,' *New York Times* (3 July 1986).

Whitehead, Andrew, 'The Jews of Kerala: Looking for Salvation,' *The Asian Age* (23 October 1996): 13.

Wiley, Susan, 'A Dying Community Saved from Obscurity,' *St. Petersburg Times* (16 October 1993): 1E. [Review of N. Katz and E. Goldberg, *The Last Jews of Cochin* (1993).]

———, 'Book on Indian Jews is Way of Remembering,' *Naples Daily News* (6 November 1993): 3D. [Review of of N. Katz and E. Goldberg, *The Last Jews of Cochin* (1993).]

Winchester, Simon, 'Whose Millennium is it Anyway?,' *Conde Nast Traveler* (March 1999): 160-1, 168-9, 214-16. [Photographs by Philip-Lorca di Corcia.]

Winter, Jana, 'Tourists Outnumber Residents in Storied Indian Community,' *Forward* (New York, 3 October 2003): 1, 22. [Reprinted as 'A View from Cochin,' *Points East* 19, no. 2 (Menlo Park, CA, July 2004): 7.]

Yehudi, Adv. Prem Doss S., 'On the Edge in Kerala,' *Ohr* (May 1987): 16-18.

———, 'Local Couple Wed in Cochin School,' *Jewish Telegraph* (Manchester, 4 July 1986): 1, 20.

———, 'The Bezalels and the "Six Bees" Nursery,' *Indian Express* 55, 216 (2 June 1987): 5.

———, 'Letter from Kerala,' *Jewish Telegraph* (Manchester, 22 July 1983): 22.

———, 'The Chinese Tiles of Cochin Jew Town Synagogue,' *Points East* 3, 1 (February 1988): 8-9.

———, 'Malayalam Play Translated into Ivrith,' *Indian Express* 56, 141 (23 March 1988): 7.

———, 'Aa Mottu Vidarunnilla (The Bud Does Not Blossom),' *Yeenad* (*This Land*) (29 May 1988): 4. [About the Kerala-born Jewish playwright, Dr. Pinhas ben Avraham Pallivathukal, who translated his Malayalam play *Theenalam* (*The Flame*) into Hebrew.] [In Malayalam.]

———, 'Tying the Bond of 3,000 Years,' *Jewish Telegraph* (9 September 1988).

———, 'Dr. Pinhas ben Abraham Pallivathukal (Obituary),' *Ohr* 26 (June 1989): 14-15.

———, 'How Poet Pinhas found an Indian Summer in Israel,' *Jewish Telegraph* 40, 43 (6 October 1989): 13.

———, *The Shingly Hebrews* (Trivandrum: Sachethana, 5750/ 1990).

———, 'Bleak Future for Jews in Kerala,' *Jewish Telegraph* (6 September 1991): 22-3.

———, 'Jewish Festive Season,' *Indian Express Sunday Magazine* (27 September 1992): 10.

———, 'Sukkoth Festival in Kochi,' *Malabar Herald* (10-17 October 1992): 3.

Zielenziger, Michael, 'A Fading Jewish Enclave in India,' *Philadelphia Inquirer* (15 September 1996).

FILMS

Agadat Kots'in (Jerusalem: Israel Film Service, 1988/1980). videocassette, 29 mins.

Chadha, Arun, *The Last To Sail* (Delhi: Doordarshan, 1993).

Jews of Cochin (Bombay: Bombay Broadcasting Network, n.d.).

Shah, Chetan, *Next Year in Jerusalem: A Film about the Jews of Cochin* (Madras: Cintel Communications, 1990).

Shalom Nehemyah (Yerushalayim: Kol Yisra'el, 1991/1978), 2 sound cassettes.

Spector, Johanna, *About the Jews of India: Cochin* (16 mm., 80 mins., Clarksburg, NJ: Alden Films, 1976).

———, 'Two Thousand Years of Freedom and Honor: The Cochin Jews' (16 mm., 80 mins., 1992, distributed by Ergo Media).

———, '2000 Years of Freedom and Honor: The Cochin Jews of India' (Teaneck, NJ: Ergo Media, 2000), 1 videocassette, 80 minutes. VHS tape, colour. Originally produced in 1992. [Explores the religious, cultural and economic life of the Cochin Jews.]

CHAPTER 3

The Bene Israel

PRIMARY DOCUMENTS AND MEMOIRS

Among primary documents concerning the Bene Israel are census reports, a few liturgical pieces and synagogue anniversary publications. Also interesting is the Chief Rabbinate of Israel's affirmation of their status as Jews (Nissim 1962).

Anonymous, *Why I Am a Jew?* (Bombay: 1895). [In Marathi.]

———, 'Marriage and Intermarriage,' *On Being Jewish, Indian and Women* 5 (December 1998): 7-10.

———, *50th Anniversary, Jewish Welfare Association: New Delhi, 1949-1999 (Judah Hyam Synagogue)* (New Delhi: no publisher, 1999).

———, 'All India Conference,' *Kol India* 15, no. 1 (Mumbai, May 2005): 9-11. [About All-India Jewish Seminar held on 30 January 2005).]

Bhende, Ashe S. and Ralphy E. Jhirad, *Demographic and Socio-Economic Characteristics of Jews in India* (Mumbai: O.R.T. India, 1997).

Binjekara, Abrahama Reubena, *Satakavali: Ingraji tarakhansaha 100 varshace Israeli pañcanga* (Mumbai: Nirnaya Press, 1911). [In Marathi.]

David, Esther, *The Walled City* (Chennai: Manas/East West Books, 1997). [Autobiographical novel about a Jewish woman's life in Ahmedabad.]

———, 'The Walled City,' *The Hindu* (4 April 1997). [Excerpts from the novel.]

———, *By the Sabarmati* (New Delhi: Penguin, 1999). [A novel.]

———, *Book of Esther* (Delhi: Viking, 2002). [A novel.]

Delman, Carmit, *Burnt Bread and Chutney: Memoir of an Indian Jewish Girl* (New York: One World, 'A Ballantine Book,' 2002).

Fischel, Walter J., 'Introduction' to *The Haggadah shel Pesach in Marathi of the Bene-Israel* (New York: Orphan Hospital Ward of Israel, 1968).

Ghosalkar, Yitshak Shelmoh and Ya'akov Yehezkel Pinglei, *Me-Hodu li-Yerushalayim: Sipur Shene Masa'ot me-Hodu le'Eretz ha-Kodesh shel Yehudim me-'adat 'Bene Yisra'el* (Jerusalem: Hotsa'at 'Tsiyon', 1993. [In Hebrew and Marathi.]

Haeems, Nina, comp. & ed., 'Essay on Religious Customs,' *Kol India* 8, 1 (Mumbai, December 1998): 17, 20.

———, *Rebecca Reuben: Scholar, Educationist, Community Leader, 1889-1957* (Mumbai: Vacha Trust, 2000).

———, *Jewish, Indian and Women: Stories from the Bene Israel Community* (Mumbai: Vacha Women's Resource Center, 2002).

Jacob, E.M., ed., *The Indo-Israel Review* (Mumbai: Zionist Association, Yom Kippur 5750/1990 issue).

Jacob, Elojah, Reuben Samuel and Leora Ezekiel, *Jewish Landmarks in Bombay & Thane* (Mumbai: Jewish Religious Union, no date [1999]).

Kollet, Shimeon, comp., *Madrikh 'tikhse Bene Yisrael = A Guide to Bene Israel Ceremonies* (Lod, Israel, Shimeon Kollet, 2001). [203 pages, in vocalized Hebrew, with instructions in English.]

———, *Guide to Bene Israel Ceremonies* (Lod, Israel: Privately published, no date [*c.* 2001]).

London Society for Promoting Christianity Amongst the Jews, *Extract of the Report of the Committee of the LSPCAJ, with Dr. Buchanan's Speech as the State of the Jews in the East* (Brooklyn: Thomas Kirk, 1811).

Maghen Hassidim Synagogue Souvenir Programme (Bombay: Maghen Hassidim Synagogue, 1976).

Moses, Ezra, *The Reform Jewish Movement in India* (Bombay: The Jewish Religious Union, n.d. [1999]).

Nissim, Itzhak, *Benei Yisrael: Piskei Halakhah [Bene Israel: Halakhic*

Decision and the Sources for the Investigation of their Laws and the Question of their Origins] (Jerusalem: Chief Rabbinate of Israel, 1962). [In Hebrew.]

On Being Jewish, Indian & Women (An Occasional Communication). Mumbai, no. 1: September 1997, no. 2: January 1998.

ORT India, *Jewish Education Resource Centre Library Subject Catalogue* (Bombay: ORT India, 1993).

Samuel, Flora, *Sanskruti Sangam* (autobiography), (Dadar, Mumbai: Jai Mulkhar Printing Press, 1996). [In Marathi.]

Sha'are Rason Synagogue, 1840-1968: A Brief Retrospect (Bombay: David Judah Samuel Pugaonkar, 1975).

Shaar Harahamim Gate if Mercy Synagogue Bi-Centenary Celebrations, 1796-Shalom-1996, Souvenir (Bombay: Shaar Harahamim Synagogue, 12 May 1996).

Shirkolkar, Mary, 'Thirty-Eight Years in Government Service,' *On Being Jewish, Indian and Women* 5 (December 1998): 5-7.

Solomon, Sam, 'The Way It Was: Some Recollections of Dr. Sam Solomon,' *On Being Jewish, Indian and Women* 5 (December 1998): 2-4.

Succath Shelomo Synagogue, Golden Jubilee Souvenir, 1921-1971 (Poona: Succath Shelomo Synagogue, 1971).

Succath Shelomo Synagogue, Platinum Jubilee Year, 1921-1996 (Pune: Succath Shelomo Synagogue, 1996).

Yigdal: Our Pune Jewish News Letter. Pune: Ohel David Synagogue (Pune, India), Monthly vol. I, no. 1, March 2000.

INCIDENTAL REFERENCES/RELATED SUBJECTS

Sinclair, W.F., 'Notes on Castes in the Dekhan,' *The Indian Antiquary* 3 (February 1874): 44-6.

SCHOLARLY STUDIES OF THE BENE ISRAEL

The Bene Israel, located in and around Bombay, are the most accessible of India's Jews as well as the most numerous. For these reasons, they have been widely studied, and we are very fortunate to have four excellent books about them by Kehimkar (1937), Strizower (1971), Isenberg (1988) and Roland (1989, 2nd edn. 1998). A fine exhibition catalogue was edited by Weil (1981). Historical writings by Bene Israel authors are noted in Chapter 3.

One topic about Which Western scholarship has become especially enamoured is the caste distinctions within the Bene Israel community, first analysed by Strizower (1971) and the subject of extended debate in the many reviews her book ignited. Caste was also the topic of articles by Strizower (1959, 1961, 1964), Newman (1972, 1975) and Weil (1979).

There have been few scholarly treatments of the Bene Israel *minhag*. Barber (1989) discussed Passover, Weil described weddings (1977) and the important role of Eliahu Hanabi in their religious life (1978), and Gussin (1971) described the *malida* rite—but his paper was not obtainable. Isenberg (1988) provided by far the most complete account of their observances. Fischel (1971/2) commented upon their literary activities. Relations with Christian missionaries was the topic of an amusing article by Isenberg (1986), and some of the missionaries themselves left important studies of the Bene Israel (Lord 1894, 1907, 1910). Commonalities with Parsis (Modi 1907/8, Schermerhorn 1978) and Muslims (Reissner 1949) have also been viewed. Their adaptation to life in Israel was discussed by Strizower (1966) and Weil (1977).

Barber, Ezekiel, *The Bene-Israel of India: Images and Reality* (Washington: University Press of America, 1981).

———, 'The Bene-Israel of India,' *Women's League Outlook* (Winter 1981): 9-10, 19-21.

———, 'Passover Observance Through the Ages by the Bene Israel of India,' *Kol Bina* 7, 1 (April 1989): 11-12.

Chandrasekhar, Sripati, 'Review of Isenberg (1988),' *Population Review* 39, 1 & 2 (1995): 122-4.

Cohen, Percy, 'Review of S. Strizower, *The Bene Israel of Bombay* (1971),' *Man* 7, 4 (1972): 673-4.

Cowen, Ida G., 'Bene Israel and M'dinat Israel,' *The Reconstructionist* 30, 5 (17 April 1964): 12-20.

Daniel, Saul, 'A Study of Bene Israel Ethnicity in India and England,' B.A. thesis, University of Nottingham (England), May 1996.

Egorova, Yulia, 'The Home of One's Own: Indian Jewish Fiction and the Problem of Bene Israel Identity,' *Journal of Indo-Judaic Studies* (Saskatoon) 6 (2003): 71-8.

David, Esther, 'Sari-Sutra: Bene Israel Costumes,' in Shalva Weil, ed., *India's Jewish Heritage: Ritual, Art, & Life-Cycle* (Mumbai: Marg Publications, 2002): 91-9.

Desai, Anita, 'Jews, Indians, and Imperialists,' *The New York Review of Books* (6 December 1990): 53-5. [Review of Isenberg, *India's Bene Israel: A Comprehensive Inquiry and Sourcebook* (1988), and Roland, *Jews in British India* (1989).]

Falber, Mosheh, *Yahadut Hodu* (Jerusalem: Misrad ha-hinukh veha-tarbut, Merkaz ha-hasbarah, 1990). [In Hebrew.]

Fischel, Walter J., 'Introduction' to *The Haggadah shel Pesach in Marathi of the Bene-Israel* (New York: Orphan Hospital Ward of Israel, 1968).

———, 'The Literary Activities of the "Bene-Israel" in India,' *Jewish Book Annual* 29 (1971-2): 5-11.

Fischel, Walter J., Shirley B. Isenberg, and Benjamin J. Israel, 'Bene Israel,' in *Encyclopaedia Judaica Yearbook* (Jerusalem: Keter, 1975/6): 244-7.

Geller, Yaakov, 'These are the names of *"Benei Yisrael"* : The Benei Yisrael Community of India,' *Bar-Ilan University's Parashat Hashavua Study Center* (Ramat Aviv) (17 January 2004). http://www.biu.ac.il/JH/parasha/shemot/gel1.html

Gussin, Carl Mark, 'Malida: A Traditional Bene Israel Ritual.' Paper read at Convention for Maharashtrian Studies, Minneapolis, MN, 1971.

———, 'The Bene Israel of India: Politics, Religion, and Systematic Change' (Ph.D. dissertation, Syracuse University, 1972).

Guy, Cynthia A., 'The Bene Israel Indian Community of Midbarit, Israel' (Ph.D. dissertation in Anthropology, University of Chicago, 1984).

Isenberg, Shirley Berry, 'The Jews of India: Collating the Data and Suggestions for Further Research,' in Thomas A. Timberg, ed., *Jews in India* (New Delhi: Vikas, 1986): 48-58.

———, 'Paradoxical Outcome of Meeting of Bene Israel and Christian Missionaries in Nineteenth Century India,' in Thomas A. Timberg, ed., *Jews in India* (New Delhi: Vikas, 1986): 348-60.

———, *India's Bene Israel: A Comprehensive Inquiry and Sourcebook* (Bombay: Popular Prakashan; and Berkeley, CA: Judah L. Magnes Museum, 1988).

———, 'The Bene Israel Villagers of Kolaba District: Generations, Culture Change, Changing Identity,' in Nathan Katz, ed., *Studies of Indian-Jewish Identity* (New Delhi: Manohar, 1995): 85-115.

———, 'The Kaifeng Jews and India's Bene Israel: Different Paths,' in Jonathan Goldstein, ed., *The Jews of China*, vol. I: *Historical and Comparative Perspectives* (Armonk NY: M.E. Sharpe, 1999): 87-103.

Jain, Ravindra K., 'Review of S. Strizower, *The Bene Israel of Bombay* (1971),' *Jewish Journal of Sociology* 15 (1973): 126-7.

Johnson, Barbara C., 'Bene Israel of India,' in Michael Terry, ed., *Reader's Guide to Judaism* (Chicago: Dearborn, 2000): 67-8.

Joel, Saul, 'In an Attempt to Understand the Social and Cultural Life of the Bene Israel Population of Dimona with Emphasis upon the Subject of Alcoholism,' unpublished report presented to the Ministry of Labour and Social Welfare, Israel, 1978.

Jones, Edward B., 'Review of J.G. Roland, *Jews in British India* (1989),' *South Asia in Review* 14, 2-3 (1990): 15-16.

Joseph, Brenda, 'Samaji's Synagogue: Tales and Traditions,' in Thomas A. Timberg, ed., *Jews in India* (New Delhi: Vikas, 1986): 361-6.

Katz, Nathan, 'Review of S.B. Isenberg, *India's Bene Israel* (1988),' *Religious Studies Review* 16, 4 (October 1990): 362-3.

Kehimkar, Haeem Samuel, *History of the Bene-Israel of India* (Tel Aviv: Dayag Press, 1937 [1897]).

Loeb, Laurence D., 'Review of S. Strizower, *The Bene Israel of Bombay* (1971),' *American Anthropologist* 75, 2 (1973): 434-6.

Lord, Rev. J. Henry, *The Jewish Mission Field in the Bombay Diocese . . . together with other Supplementary Matters* (Bombay: Education Society's Stream Press, 1894).

———, *The Jews in India and the Far East* (Kolhapur: The Mission Press, 1907). [Reprint, Westport, CT: Greenwood Press, 1976.]

———, *Israel, God's Inheritance: Some Words of a Friend, Addressed, Primarily, to the Bene-Israel of the Bombay Presidency* (Kolhapur: The Mission Press, 1910).

———, 'Bene-Israel,' in James Hastings, ed., *Encyclopaedia of Religion and Ethics* (New York: Charles Scribner's Sons, rpt. 1958 [1908]): II, 469-74.

Masliyah, Sadok, 'The Bene Israel and the Baghdadis: Two Indian Jewish Communities in Conflict,' *Judaism* 43/3 (Summer 1994): 279-93.

Mayers, Gabriel Simon, 'Jewish Religious Discrimination and the Bene Israel Jews in India and Israel,' (M.A. thesis, Western Washington University, 2001), v + 134 pp.

Menasseh, Sara, 'The Music of the Bene Israel Jews of Bombay,' in Yuvel Shaked, producer, *Eliyahoo Hanabee* [CD] Feher Jewish Music Center, Tel Aviv: Beth Hatefutsoth. [Catalogue number BTR 0101.]

Modi, Shams ul-ulma Jivanji Jamshedi, 'Kiss of Peace among the Bene Israels of Bombay and the Hamâzor among the Parsees,' *Journal of the Anthropological Society of Bombay* 8, 2 (1907-8): 84-95.

Musleah, Rabbi Ezekiel N., 'There Are Jews Everywhere,' *Judaism* 21, 82 (Spring 1972): 244-7. [Review of S. Strizower, *The Bene Israel of Bombay*, 1971).]

Needel, Yale, 'The Jews as a Caste,' unpublished senior religion thesis, Muhlenberg College, Allentown PA, 1998.

Ness, Brenda Joseph, 'The Children of Jacob: The Bene Israel of Maharashtra' (Ph.D. dissertation, University of California at Los Angeles, 1996).

Newman, Robert S., 'Caste and the Indian Jews,' *Indian Journal of Sociology* 3, 1 & 2 (1972): 35-54.

———, 'Caste and the Indian Jews,' *The Eastern Anthropologist* 28, 3 (1975): 195-213.

Numark, Mitch, 'Constructing a Jewish Nation in Colonial India: History, Narratives of Descent, and the Vocabulary of Modernity,' *Jewish Social Studies* (Bloomington, IN) 7, 2 (2001): 89-113.

Palgi, Phyllis, and Rosalind O'Brien, 'The Bene Israel Community: Excerpt from a Study,' *Israel Yearbook* (1972): 161-8.

Pamm, A.N., 'The Services of the Bene Israel of India in the Bombay Army,' *The Orders and Medals Research Society* 33, 4 (1994): 332-40.

Rao, R. Raj, *Nissim Ezekiel: The Authorized Biography* (New Delhi: Viking, by Penguin Books India, 2000).

———, 'A Profiler of Our Conscience,' *The Age on Sunday* (7 May 2000). [About Nissim Ezekiel.]

———, 'The Jewish Background of Nissim Ezekiel's Poetry,' *Journal of Indo-Judaic Studies* 5 (Saskatoon) (June 2002): 7-28.

Reissner, H.G., 'The Ummi Prophet and the Banu Israil of the Qur'an,' *The Muslim World* 39 (1949): 276-81.

Reuben, Joseph N., *The Co-operative Movement: Considered with Special Reference to the Bene-Israel* (Bombay: n.p., 1921).

Ribeiro, Victor Rangel, 'Jews in British India: An Authoritative Study Based on Personal Interviews,' *News India* (11 January 1991): 30. [Review of J.G. Roland, *Jews in British India* (1989).]

Richman, Paula, 'Review of Esther David, *The Walled City*, 1997,' *Journal of Indo-Judaic Studies* 5 (Saskatoon) (June 2002): 81-3.

Rodriguz, Aron, 'Review of J.G. Roland, *Jews in British India* (1989),' *The American Historical Review* 96, 1 (February 1991): 245-6.

Roland, Joan G., 'Bene Israel and Baghdadi Jews of Bombay: Communal and National Identities.' Paper read at the Duquense History Forum, Pittsburgh, October 1978.

———, 'Modern Bombay Jewry: Bene Israel Communal Activity,

1880-1930.' Paper read at the Association of Jewish Studies Meeting, Boston, December 1979.

———, 'The Jews of India: Communal Survival or the End of a Sojourn?,' *Jewish Social Studies* 42, 1 (1980): 75-90.

———, 'A Decade of Vitality: Bene Israel Communal Development (1917-1927),' in Thomas A. Timberg, ed., *Jews in India* (New Delhi: Vikas, 1986): 285-347.

———, *Jews in British India: Identity in a Colonial Era* (Hanover and London: University Press of New England, 1989).

———, 'Indian-Jewish Identity of the Bene Israel during the British Raj.' Paper read at the annual meeting of the American Academy of Religion, New Orleans, LA, 19 November 1990.

———, 'Indian-Jewish Identity of the Bene Israel during the British Raj,' in Nathan Katz, ed., *Studies of Indian-Jewish Identity* (New Delhi: Manohar, 1995): 117-31.

———, 'Adaptation and Identity among Second-Generation Indian Jews in Israel,' *Jewish Journal of Sociology* 37, 1 (1995): 5-37.

———, 'The Bene Israel in Israel: An Overview,' *Population Review* 39, 1 & 2 (1995): 66-73.

———, 'The Transformation of Indian Identity among Bene Israel in Israel,' in Frederick Lazin and Gregory Mahler, eds., *Israel in the Nations* (Gainesville: University Press of Florida, 1996): 169-93.

———, 'Jews in India Today: A Community Survives,' *Pe'amim* 71 (1997): 94-120. [In Hebrew.]

———, *The Jewish Communities of India: Identity in a Colonial Era* (New Brunswick and London: Transaction Publishers, 1998).

———, 'Religious Observances of the Bene Israel: Persistence and the Refashioning of Tradition,' *Journal of Indo-Judaic Studies* (Saskatoon) 3 (2000): 22-47.

———, ' "She Taught from the Heart": The Life and Legacy of a Bene Israel Educator', in Rebec Reuben, ed., *Rebecca Reuben: Scholar, Educationist, Community Leader, 1889-1957* (Mumbai: Vacha Trust, 2000), *Journal of Indo-Judaic Studies* (Saskatoon) 6 (2003): 96-102. [Review of Nina Haeems.]

Samuel, Flora, *Cultural Integration: The Life Story of Indian Jews from Israel* (Mumbai: Jaimalhar Press, 1996). [In Marathi.]

———, 'The Kirtan,' *Pe'amim* 71 (1997): 121-8. [In Hebrew.]

Strizower, Schifra, 'Jews as an Indian Caste,' *Jewish Journal of Sociology* 1, 1 (1959): 43-57.

———, 'Ten Tribes of Bombay,' *Jewish Chronicle* (London, 1 July 1961): 9-10.

———, 'Jews as an Indian Caste,' in Louis Schneider, ed., *Religion, Culture and Society* (New York: John Wiley & Sons, 1964).

———, 'The Bene Israel in Israel,' *Middle Eastern Studies* 2, 2 (January 1966): 122-43.

———, 'The Social Structure of an Indian Jewish Community,' Ph.D. dissertation, University of London, 1967.

———, *The Bene Israel of Bombay: A Study of a Jewish Community* (New York: Schocken Books, 1971).

———, *The Children of Israel: The Bene Israel of Bombay* (Oxford: Basil Blackwell, 1971).

———, 'The Bene Israel and the Jewish People,' in *Salo Wittmayer Baron Jubilee Volume* (New York: Columbia University Press, 1977): 859-86.

Tinker, Hugh, 'Indians in Israel: The Acceptance Model and Its Limitations,' *Race* 13 (1971): 81-4.

———, 'Review of S. Strizower, *The Bene Israel of Bombay* (1971),' *Race* 14 (1972): 98-100.

Toledano, Dayan Dr. Pinchas, *The Bene Israel of India* (London: Society of Heshaim, Spanish & Portuguese Jews' Congregation (n.d. [*c.* 2002]).

Venkateshwarlu, D., 'Jewish Experience in India and the Making of an Indian Jewish Novel.' Paper read at 'A View from the Margin: The State of the Art of Indo-Judaic Studies,' Oxford Centre for Hebrew and Jewish Studies, U.K., 2-6 July 2002. [Reading Esther David's *The Walled City* (1997).]

———, 'Jewish Experience in India, or the Making of an Indian Jewish Novel: A Reading of Esther David's *The Walled City*,' *Journal of Indo-Judaic Studies* (Saskatoon) 7-8 (2004-5): 122-4.

Weil, Shalva, 'Bene Israel in Britain,' *New Community* 3 (1974).

———, 'Bene Israel Indian Jews in Lod, Israel: A Study of the Persistence of Ethnicity and Ethnic Identity,' Ph.D. dissertation, University of Sussex, 1977.

———, 'Names and Identity among the Bene Israel,' *Ethnic Groups* 1 (1977): 201-19.

———, 'Verbal Interaction among the Bene Israel,' *International Journal of the Sociology of Language* 13 (1977).

———, 'Verbal Interaction among the Bene Israel,' *Linguistics* 193 (1977): 71-85.

———, 'The Wedding among Bene Israel Indian Jews in Israel,' *Abstracts: Seventh World Congress of Jewish Studies* (Jerusalem: 1977).

———, 'Eliahu Hannabi among the Bene Israel.' Paper read at the International Congress of Anthropology, New Delhi, 1978.

———, 'Caste in Israel.' Paper presented at the tenth meeting of the Israel Sociological Association, Haifa, 1979.

———, 'The State of Research into Bene Israel Indian Jews,' *The Economic and Social History Review* 18, 4 (1980).

———, ed., *The Jews from the Konkan: The Bene Israel Communities in India* (Tel Aviv: The Nahum Goldmann Museum of the Jewish Diaspora, 1981). [Exhibition catalogue.]

———, 'Contacts between the Bene Israel and the Holy Land from the 8th Century BCE until 1948: An Ethnohistorical Perspective,' in Issachar Ben-Ami, ed., *The Sephardi and Oriental Jewish Heritage* (Jerusalem: Magnus Press, 1982): 165-78.

———, 'Interpersonal Relations and Uses of Language among Bene Israel in Israel,' in Shlomo Deshen and Moshe Shokeid, eds., *Oriental Jews* (Jerusalem: Shocken, 1984): 306-11. [In Hebrew.]

———, 'Review of Benjamin J. Israel, *The Bene Israel in India: Some Studies*', in *Asian and African Studies* (1985): 131-2.

———, 'An Overview of Research on the Bene Israel,' in Thomas A. Timberg, ed., *Jews in India* (New Delhi: Vikas, 1986): 12-27.

———, 'Anthropology becomes Home: Home becomes

Anthropology,' in Anthony Jackson, ed., *Anthropology at Home* (London: Tavistock Publications, ASA Monograph No. 25, 1987): 196-212.

———, 'The Influence of Caste Ideology in Israel,' in Meir Gottesman, ed., *Cultural Transition: The Case of Immigrant Youth* (Jerusalem: n.p. 1988): 150-61.

———, ' "Proximal Households" as Alternatives to Joint Families in Israel,' in Lea Shamgar-Handelman and Rosselle Palomba, eds., *Alternative Patterns of Family Life in Modern Societies* (Roma: Consiglio della Richerche, Instituto di Recherche Sulta Popolazione, 1988 [1987]): 87-103.

———, 'Bene Israel,' in Geoffrey Wigoder, ed., *Encyclopedia of Judaism*. (Jerusalem: Jerusalem Publishing House, 1989): 109-10, 714-15.

———, 'Yom Kippur: The Festival of Closing the Doors,' in Hananya Goodman, ed., *From Jerusalem to Benares: Comparative Studies in Judaism and Hinduism* (Albany: State University of New York Press, 1994): 85-100.

———, 'The Secular and Religious Elite among the Bene Israel (Indian Jews),' *Pe'amim* (1994): 49-63. [In Hebrew.]

———, 'Bene Israel,' in Reeva S. Simon, Philip Martar, and Richard W. Bulliet, eds., *Encyclopedia of the Modern Middle East*, vol. 1 (New York: Macmillan, 1996): 350.

———, 'Religious Leadership vs. Secular Authority: The Case of the Bene Israel,' *The Eastern Anthropologist* 49, nos. 3&4 (1996): 301-16.

———, 'Bene Israel,' in R.J. Zwi Werblowsky and G. Wigoder, eds., *Oxford Dictionary of the Jewish Religion* (New York: Oxford University Press, 1997): 113.

———, 'The Bene Israel in India,' in Yuval Shaked, ed., *Eliyahoo Hanabee: The Musical Tradition of the Bene Israel of Bombay* (Tel Aviv: Beth Hatefusoth, the Museum of the Jewish Diaspora, 2001).

———, 'Research and Memory: The Case of the Bene Israel and Some Other Others.' Paper read at 'A View from the Margin: The State of the Art of Indo-Judaic Studies,' Oxford Centre

for Hebrew and Jewish Studies, U.K., 2-6 July 2002.
———, 'Bene Israel Rites and Routines,' in Shalva Weil, ed., *India's Jewish Heritage: Ritual, Art, & Life-Cycle* (Mumbai: Marg Publications, 2002): 79-89.
———, 'Review of Esther David, *The Book of Esther* (2002),' in *Biblio: A Review of Books* (New Delhi: Manohar, 2003): 26.
———, 'Motherland and Fatherland as Dichotomous Diasporas: The Case of the Bene Israel,' in Lisa Anteby, William Berthomiere and Gabriel Sheffer, eds., *Les Diasporas 2000 ans d'histoire* (Rennes: Presses Universitaires de Rennes, 2005): 91-9.
Wester, Nils, 'Bene Israel: A Jewish Community In India,' in Asko Parpola and Bent Smidt Hansen, eds., *South Asian Religion and Society* (London: Curzon Press Ltd., and Riverdale, MD: Riverdale Press, *Scandinavian Institute of Asian Studies Monograph No. 11*, 1986): 205-22.

GENERAL & NEWSPAPER ACCOUNTS OF BENE ISRAEL

Bene Israel authors have been especially prolific, and one result has been several excellent, comprehensive studies of this unique community. Especially noteworthy are Kehimkar (1937 [1897]), Shelim Samuel (1963) and B.J. Israel (1963, 1982, 1984a). Ezekiel (1948) and Reuben (1913) have made similar contributions.

Bene Israel observances in general have been described by David (1988, 1989) and F. Samuel (1986). Observances for specific holidays and events have been discussed as well: Yom Kippur (Anonymous 1984), Shabbat (Anonymous 1984), Passover (Friedman 1989; Trivedi 1990), Tisha b'Av (Kolet 1986), Tu b'Shvat (Anonymous 1984), Marriage (Samson 1917; B.J. Israel 1962; Anonymous 1984, 1988), and the veneration of the Prophet Elijah (Anonymous 1984).

The status of Bene Israel women has received attention (Walkar 1925; N. Ezekiel 1969; E.M. Jacob 1984; Jhirad 1984), as have relations with Christians (Wilson 1865, 1874, 1947), Muslims (Elijah n.d.) and Hindus (Immanuel 1989). Biographies of distinguished members of the community have been written and published regularly.

The Bene Israel community has produced outstanding writers (Anonymous 1984), including several novelists (Kurulkar 1878; Mahadevan 1971), playwrights (Elias 1984) and traditional (Anonymous 1984) as well as modern poets (Anonymous 1984, 1989; N. Ezekiel 1976, 1982; N. Anklesaria 1986).

Settlement in Israel has been studied by Cale (1952), Shore (1952), Immanuel (1989) and Gorenberg (1990). The controversy regarding the Jewish status of the Bene Israel was the subject of papers by J.B. Israel (1919), Shulewitz (1963), Anonymous (1963, 1964) and Feldman and Aaron (1986).

Abraham, A.S., 'Review of S. Strizower, *The Children of Israel* (1967),' *Times of India* (14 May 1972).

Abraham, Abraham, 'Indian Jews on the East Coast,' *desiTALK* (New York, 20 February 1998): 2.

Abraham, Ruby Rebecca, 'The Judah Compound of Jubbulpore,' *On Being Jewish, Indian and Women* 2 (January 1998): 4-5.

Abraham, Sam, 'Destruction of Holy Places,' *Free Press Journal* (no publ. data available). [Letter to the editor about Karachi synagogue.]

———, 'Synagogue Not Restored in Karachi,' *News India-Times* (New York, 16 December 1994): 54.

Ahmed, Khaleed, 'Why are the Jews "kanjoos"?,' *Daily Times* (Karachi, 21 October 2005).

Ahmed, Rashmeez, 'India's Children of Israel Find Their Roots,' *Times of India* (New Delhi, 11 July 2002).

———, 'DNA Tests Link Bene Israelis to Moses,' *The Sunday Times* (New Delhi, 21 July 2002).

Anklesaria, Havovi, ed., *Journal of Indian Writing in English* 14, 2 (July 1986). [Special Number on Nissim Ezekiel.]

Anonymous, *Curiosities of Judaism* (Bombay, 1886).
———, *Chronology of the Past Events of Jews in India* (Bombay (?): Isaac Saddock, on behalf of the Israelite Society, 1921). [In Marathi.]
———, 'The Problem of Benei Israel,' *Israel Digest of Press and Events in Israel and the Middle East* 6, 17 (16 August 1963): 6.
———, 'The Problem of the Benei Israel,' in E. Elias & E. Isaac, eds., *Jews in India with Who Is Who 1963* (Ernakulam: Indo-Israel Publications, 1964): 65-8.
———, 'A Short Biographical Sketch of Samuel Ezekiel Divekar, The First Bene-Israel to Build a Synagogue (1796),' in E.M. Jacob (1984): 27-30.
———, 'Benjamin Samson Ashtamkar: The First Kirtankar among the Bene-Israels (18-8-80),' in E.M. Jacob (1984): 31-2.
———, 'Joseph Ezekiel Rajpurkar, J.P., The First Fellow of the Bombay University (1879),' in E.M. Jacob (1984): 32-3.
———, 'Haeem Samuel Kehimkar, The First to Write an Authentic History of the Bene Israel (1897),' in E.M. Jacob (1984): 34-5.
———, 'Dr. Elijah Moses Rajpurkar, M.D.: The Only Bene-Israel Mayor (1937),' in E.M. Jacob (1984): 38-9.
———, 'Padmashri Reuben David (Dandekar): The Miracle-man of Ahmedabad Zoo,' in E.M. Jacob (1984): 66-8.
———, 'Padmashri David Abraham (Cheulkar): The Immortal Actor,' in E.M. Jacob (1984): 70-1.
———, 'Dr. (Miss) Esther Abraham Solomon (Kasookar): The First Bene-Israel Recognised Sanskrit Scholar (1948),' in E.M. Jacob (1984): 71-2.
———, 'Prof. Nissim Ezekiel (Talkar): The First Bene-Israel Poet of International Repute (1960),' in E.M. Jacob (1984): 74.
———, 'Observance of "Yom Kippur" and "Shabbath" by the Ancient Bene-Israels,' in E.M. Jacob (1984): 80-1.
———, 'A Miracle that Occurred in Tala Village: A Story Depicting a Staunch Faith in "Shema",' in E.M. Jacob (1984): 81.
———, 'Shebat 15 — New Year for Trees: Why the Bene-Israels

Adore this Festival the Most,' in E.M. Jacob (1984): 82-3.

———, 'List of Bene Israel Authors & Publications,' in E.M. Jacob (1984): 178-9.

———, *A Tribute to Gerhad Gabriel* (Bombay: ORT India, 1987).

———, 'Jewish History,' *Bombay Magazine* (7 April 1988).

———, 'A Bene Israel Marriage Custom,' *Ohr* 25 (November 1988): 15-17.

———, 'Bene Israel Jews Exist for Over 2,000 Years in India,' *Current Events* 30, 10 (16-28 February 1989): 1.

———, 'At the UFT Jewish Heritage Festival, Views of Indian Jewish Life Spice Up the Day,' *UFT Bulletin/New York Teacher* (12 June 1989).

———, 'Portrait of a Poet [Nissim Ezekiel],' *India Worldwide* (December 1989): 53.

———, 'Professor Nissim Ezekiel, Indian-Jewish Poet,' *Sephardic News International* (February 1990): 28.

———, *ORT India-JDC India: 30 Years of Service to Society* (Bombay: ORT, India, 1991).

———, 'Indian Jewish Community Celebrates Unique Event in Its History,' *News India* (New York, 13 September 1991).

———, 'B'Bay Jews Welcome Ties With Israel,' *News India* (New York, 14 February 1992): 14.

———, 'Jewish Educationist Who Dedicated Her Life to Islamic School,' *News India* (New York, 20 March 1992): 12.

———, 'Poet of Careful Craftsmanship,' *The Hindu* (Madras, 17 April 1992). [About Nissim Ezekiel.]

———, 'The Jews of India Thru Joan Roth's Camera Lens' & 'Keeping A Different Faith While Following Local Customs In India,' *News India* (New York, 4 December 1992): 28.

———, 'Sole Survivor,' *Brooklyn Jewish Press* (7 May 1993): 63. [About Karachi community.]

———, 'From Israel to City on Memory Lane,' *Indian Express* (24 May 1993): 3. [About Dr. E.M. Best.]

———, 'A Mikveh in Bombay,' *Brooklyn Jewish Press* (25 June 1993): 70.

———, 'The Jews of Delhi,' *India Global* (July 1993): 12.

———, 'A Happy Rosh Hashanah for Indian Jews,' *News India-Times* (New York, 24 September 1993): 14.

———, 'Oldest Synagogue to Mark Bicentennial,' *News India-Times* (New York, 18 February 1994): 20.

———, 'We've Never Ever Felt Anti-Semitism in India,' *News India-Times* (New York, 15 April 1994): 52.

———, 'City Synagogues' (editorial), *Times of India* (22 August 1994).

———, 'American Dream,' *The Afternoon Dispatch & Courier* (20 October 1994): 9. [About John Perry.]

———, 'A Bombay Boy Comes Home to Repay a Debt,' *Brooklyn Jewish Press* (9 June 1995): 84. [About John Perry.]

———, 'Succath Synagogue Celebrates 74th Anniversary,' *Maharashtra Herald* (Pune, 12 June 1995).

———, 'Jews Celebrate,' *Times of India* (Ahmedabad, 18 August 1997): 16.

———, 'ORT India Praised, Recognized by the Bombay Jewish Community,' *Brooklyn Jewish Press* (10 April 1998): 32.

———, 'UFTers learn of Jewish Delhi,' *New York Teacher* 40, no. 22 (16 June 1999): 25.

———, 'Rosh Hashana and Yom Kippur Services Being Held by the Indian Jewish Community in Manhattan,' *Jewish Press* (Brooklyn, 27 August 1999): 30.

———, 'A Member of the Congregation blows a *shofar*. . .' *Times of India* (13 September 1999): 5. [Photo.]

———, 'Jews all Over the World Observe "The Day of Atonement" from Sins,' *Times of India* (20 September 1999): 3.

———, 'Shofar So Good,' *Times of India* (Thane Plus), (2 January 2000): 1.

———, 'Window on India: First Jewish Community Center in Bombay Opens with Flurry of Activity,' *American Joint Distribution Committee News and Features* (18 January 2000) http://www.jdc.org/news/india/html

———, 'Indian Jews hope for Closer Indo-Israel Ties,' *Times of India* (New Delhi, 4 September 2003).

———, ' "Maharashtra Day" in Israel,' *Times of India* (3 May

2005).http://timesofindia.indiatimes.com/articleshow/1095781.cms

Anshel, Aharon ben, 'Review of C. Delman, *Burnt Bread and Chutney* (2002),' in *Jewish Press* (Brooklyn, 17 January 2003): 83.

Asher, Uma, 'Indian Food, Music and Games Lent Cheer to Jewish Festival of Lights,' *Times of India* (10 December 1996): 3.

Balakrishnan, Ramgopal, 'After the Exodus, A Place to Call One's Own,' *The Sunday Observer* (21-7 July 1991).

Balaram, Gunvanthi, 'The "masjid" that Samuel Divekar Built,' *Sunday Times of India* (19 May 1996): 5.

———, 'Jews Herald in New Year with Traditional Fervor,' *Times of India* (Mumbai, 3 October 1997): 5.

Banerjee, Mita, 'Judaism: A Way of Life,' *Pune Newsline* (24 April 1998): 3.

Barber, Ezekiel, 'The Bene-Israel of India,' *Reform Judaism* (Summer 1982): 8.

Bene Israel Cookbook (Bombay: Sisterhood of the Jewish Religious Union, 1986).

Benjamin (Gadkar), Daniel Elijah, 'Succath Shelomo Synagogue Celebrates 77th Anniversary,' *Pune Herald* (17 May 1998): 2.

Blustain, Sarah, 'A Grandmother's Secrets,' *Lilith* (Spring 2003): 36. [Review of Carmit Delman, *Burnt Bread and Chutney: A Memoir of an Indian Jewish Girl* (2002).]

Boykin, James H., *Beta, Bene, and the Periphal Diaspora* (Miami: James H. Boykin, 1990): 43-52 [Ch IV, 'Bene Israel and the Cochin Jews'.]

Cale, Ruth, 'The Case of Indian Jews Who Wanted to Return,' *Israel Speaks* (25 January 1952): 2.

Chambers, Steve, 'Indian Jews Bask in Their Survival,' *Star-Ledger* (NJ, 13 December 1998): 25, 32

Choudhury, Panna Roy, 'Bayiti: A Secure Haven for the Aged,' *Free Press Journal* (8 November 1997).

Crosette, Barbara, 'Sense of Solitude and Fear of a Backlash Trouble Bombay Jews,' New York *Times* (17 February 1991).

Dandekar, B.B., *Bene Israel Tales* (Lawrence, KS: A.B. Literary House, 1991). [Short stories.]

———, *David Rahabi* (Lawrence, KS: A.B. Literary House, 1993). [Novel.]

Daniel, Samuel M., Joseph Moses and Elizabeth Naidu, 'Elijah E. Jhirad: A Profile,' *Kol Bina* 7, 2 (1989): 9-43.

Datta, Jyotirmoy, 'A Brief History of an Ancient Indian Jewish Group,' *India Abroad* (5 April 1996): 48.

David, Reuben, ed., *Ahmedabad Zoo* (Ahmedabad: Municipal Corporation, n.d. [*c.* 1975]).

David, Flt. Lt. Nagavkar Asher (Retd.), *Jewish Holidays and Rituals* (Bombay: The Author, 1988).

———, *Hebrew (Jewish) Rituals with English Alphabets* (Bombay: The Author, 1989).

David, N.E., 'Judaism (2nd Paper),' in *Convention of Religions in India (Report of the First Convention of Religions in India 1909)* (Delhi: Bimla Publishing House, 1982 [1909]): 52-9.

Divekar, Ezekiel Solomon, *The Life of Haeem Solomon Kehimkar* (Bombay: Moshe Avraham Gadkar, 1923). [In Marathi.]

D'Silva, Anthony, 'Shalom, Old Friends,' *The Afternoon on Sunday* (22 November 1992): 6, 22.

Elias, A., 'Joseph David Penkar (1879-1949), Script-writer for the First Indian Talkie: Alam Ara (1929),' in E.M. Jacob (Gadkar), *The Religious and Cultural History of the Bene Israels of India* (1984): 69-70.

Elijah, Samuel H., 'Tipu Sultan and the Bene-Israel of India,' *JPJH* (n.d.): 1428-30.

———, 'Notes on the Bene-Israels,' *JPJH* (n.d.): 1548.

Ezekiel, Gulu, 'Shimon Gets a Warm Shalom at Synagogue,' *Pioneer* (New Delhi, 18 May 1993).

Ezekiel, Joe, 'From One Synagogue to 20,' *India Abroad* (New York, 10 January 1992): 18.

Ezekiel, Moses, *History and Culture of the Bene Israel of India* (Bombay: Nadia, 1948).

Ezekiel, Dr. (Mrs.) Nancy, 'The Jewish Women of India,' *Indian*

Jewish Year Book (Bombay: Privately published, 1969): 37-43.

Ezekiel, Nissim, *Hymns in Darkness* (Delhi: Oxford University Press, 1976).

———, *Latter-Day Psalms* (Delhi: Oxford University Press, 1982).

———, *Collected Poems* (Delhi: Oxford University Press, 1989).

———, 'Jewish Wedding in Bombay,' *The Indian-American* (November 1992). [Poem.]

Farrell, Paul, 'India-based Judaism Lives on in Rego Park,' *Times/Ledger* (10 December 1998): 5, 27.

Feldman, Rachel, and Susan Aaron, 'The Bene Israel: Persisting Misconceptions of Status,' *Kol Bina* 6, 1 (September 1986): 7-9.

Fiahkoff, Rachel, 'A Wedding in Jacob's Circle: India's Bene-Israel Jews Maintain Tradition,' *Jewish World* (16-22 December 1994): 33, 37.

Fishkoff, Sue, 'A Story of Survival,' *Points East* 10, 1 (March 1995): 1, 4-5. [Reprint from *Jerusalem Post Magazine* (9 July 1993).]

Freund, Michael, 'Bene Israel Rabbi Returns to Indian Community,' *Jerusalem Post Online Edition* (27 May 2004).

Friedman, Beatrice I., 'Seder in India,' *Kol Bina* 7, 1 (April 1989): 13-14.

Friel, Terry, 'Migration Saps Ancient Indian Jewish Town,' *South Florida Sun-Sentinel* (Ft. Lauderdale, 21 March 2003): 5E.

Gadkar, Mrs. Rachel, 'Two Bene-Israel Personalities who Enlightened the Illiterates in the 19th Century,' in Jacob (1984): 61-3.

———, 'Status and Activities of Bene-Israels in Old Bombay,' in Jacob (1984): 144-5.

Gadkar, Rachel, Moses Isaac Pezarkar, Lemuel M. Solomon, Norman Elijah, David N. Haeems, Lily Moses Reuben Korlekar, Ruby Samuel, and Hannan Isaiah Shapurkar, 'Open Debate: What is the Future of Conducting Prayers in Synagogues,' *Kol India* 13, no. 3 (Mumbai: March 2004): 4-5, 28.

Gadkari, Madhav, *Bene Israel: People and Country* (Mumbai: International Marathi Society, 1996). [In Marathi.]

Gaon, Baz, 'Salam Bombay,' *Ma'ariv Supplement* (Tel Aviv) (20 February 2004): 32-8. [In Hebrew.]

Ghosh, Bina, 'Trained at School,' *Times of India* (Bombay, 15 January 1992): 2. [About ORT.]

———, 'Faraway from the "Promised Land",' *The Independent* (26 March 1992).

Goodman, Matthew, 'How a Shipwreck Begat a Sweet-and-Spicy Cuisine,' *The Forward* (17 August 2001): 13. [About Bene Israel cuisine.]

Gitlin, Jason, 'UJA Campaign Director Sees Dollars at Work Helping Jews of India,' *MW Jewish News* (1 May 1997): 12-14.

Goldberg, Ellen Israel, 'Ben Tzion is One of a Kind : Indian-Israeli Artist Brings the Best of Both Worlds,' *India Worldwide* (January 1995): 8-10.

Goldfarb, Jack, 'Doing the Rite Thing in Bombay,' *Jewish News* (April 1992).

Goldman, Merle, 'Local Couple to Strengthen Judaism in Bombay,' *Washtenaw Jewish News* (Ann Arbor, MI) (October 1989): 1, 12.

Gorenberg, Gershom, 'An Israeli Indian Tribe: A Successful Transplant,' *Hadassah Magazine* (January 1990): 18-21.

Green, David B., 'The Patriot: Indian Poet Nissim Ezekiel is a Man of Many Loyalties,' *Jerusalem Report* (13 July 1995): 46.

Gross, David C., 'To Live or To Die? Yom Kippur Ruling Awaits President; Former Leader of Indian Jewish Community appeals to Ford for Political Asylum in America,' *New York Jewish Week* (3-9 October 1976): 1, 32.

Gupta, Shekhar, 'Israel: An Indian Enclave,' *India Today* (15 April 1992): 100-1.

Halperin, Alex, 'A Small World Weds Saris and Yarmulkes,' *Forward* (New York, 28 November 2003), p. 16.

Harrison, Donald M., 'Shalom, Bombay,' *San Diego Jewish Press* (13 March 1998): 8-10, 20.

Hassenfeld, Sylvia, and Theodore Comet, 'First JDC President's Mission to India: A Voyage of Discovery,' *JDC Report to the Board* (2/19/91).

Hillstedt, Leone McGregor, 'Jerusha Jhirad,' in *Women Physicians of the World: Autobiographies of Medical Pioneers* (Washington and London: Hemisphere Publishing Corp., McGraw Hill Book Co., n.d.): 65-7.

Immanuel, Jon, 'Builders of Israel: Israel's Indian Community,' *Jerusalem Post* (10 May 1989): 8-10.

———, 'Jews in a Hindu Society,' *Jerusalem Post* (10 May 1989): 10.

Indian Jewish Year Book (Bombay, 1969).

Israel, Benjamin J., *Khan Bahadur Jacob Bapuji Israel, a Personal Sketch* (Bombay: G.G. Pathere, 1960).

———, 'The Problem of Marriage for the Bene Israel in Israel,' *Mebasser* (Bombay, June 1962): 9.

———, *Religious Evolution among the Bene Israel of India Since 1750* (Bombay: Privately published, 1963).

———, *The Jews of India* (New Delhi: Centre for Jewish and Inter-Faith Studies, Jewish Welfare Association, 1982. [Reprinted New Delhi: Mosaic Books, 1998.]

———, *The Bene Israel of India: Some Studies* (New York: Apt Books, and Delhi: Orient Longman, 1984a).

———, 'The Jews Who Came to Stay,' *Weekend Telegraph* (Calcutta, 13 October 1984b).

Israel, Jacob B., *Letters of the Bene Israel Community of British India* (Bombay, 1917, 1918).

———, A.S. Erulkar et al., *The Bene Israel Conference Imbroglio* (Bombay, 1917).

———, *Reflections on the Purity or Otherwise of the Bene Israel Race of India* (Bombay: Bahadur Printing Works, 1919).

Jacob, Elijah, Reuben Samuel, and Leora Ezekiel, *Jewish Landmarks in Bombay City* (Bombay: J.R.U. Youth Group, 1991).

———, eds., *Jewish Landmarks in Bombay & Thane* (Bombay: J.R.U. Youth Group, 2000).

Jacob, Ezekiel Moses (Gadkar), *The Religious and Cultural History of the Bene Israels of India, 'Gate of Mercy' Synagogue*, 2 vols. (Bombay: E.M. Jacob Gadkar for 'Gate of Mercy' Synagogue, 1984). [Book I Photographs; Book II Text.]

———, 'History of "Shaar Harahamin—Gate of Mercy" Synagogue,' in Jacob (1984): 1-10.

———, 'Bombay and the Bene-Israels during the 17th, 18th and 19th Century,' in Jacob (1984): 84-90.

———, 'History of the Bene-Israels,' in Jacob (1984): 96-102.

———, 'Bene-Israel Women,' in Jacob (1984): 169-71.

———, 'India's Jews,' letter to the editor, *Jerusalem Post* (18 September 1989): 4.

Jhirad, Elijah, 'Bene Israel's Judaism was Never in Question,' *Philadelphia Jewish Exponent* (8 July 1994): 20. [Letter to the editor.]

Jhirad, Dr. Jerusha J., 'Autobiography of . . . the First Woman to Secure Government Scholarship Meant for Men Only (1914) and the First Indian Chief Medical Officer, Cama and Albert Hospital (1928),' in *The Religious and Cultural History of the Bene Israels of India*, 'Gate of Mercy' Synagogue, 2 vols. (Bombay: EM. Jacob Gadkar for 'Gate of Mercy' Synagogue, 1984).

Johnson, Mark, 'Living as Indian Jews in America,' *Pioneer* (29 August 1993): 6-7.

Journal of Indian Writing in English, The (Special Number on Nissim Ezekiel), ed. Havovi Anklesaria, 14, 2 (July 1986).

Judah Hyam Hall Silver Jubilee 5717-5742 (1956/57-1981/82) (New Delhi, 1982).

Judah Hyam Synagogue, *50th Anniversary Jewish Welfare Association-New Delhi (1949-1999)* (New Delhi: Judah Hyam Synagogue, no date [1999]).

Kail, Shila, 'The Kosher Menu,' *Afternoon on Sunday* (Mumbai, 26 April 1998): 15-16.

Kamdar, Neema, 'Dead End,' *Sunday Mid-Day* (6 March 1994): 8-9.

Kamerleker, Moses Elijah, *The Power of Tithe or Deeds not Words; God Helps Those Who Help Themselves* (Simla: Examiner's Office, Military Works, 1917).

Karp, Jonathan, 'Seeking Lost Tribes of Israel in India, Using DNA Testing,' *Wall Street Journal* (11 May 1998): 1f.

Kavarana, Roxanne, 'Shanah Tovah!,' *Sunday Times of India* (Mumbai, 12 September 1999): 6.

Kazmin, Amy Louise, 'The Lure of the Unfamiliar,' *Jerusalem Report* (11 December 1997): 46-7. [Review of Esther David, *The Walled City* (1997).]

Kehimkar, Haeem Samuel, *Sketch of the History of the Beni-Israel and an Appeal for their Education* (Bombay, *c.* 1865).

———. *History of the Bene-Israel of India* (Tel Aviv: Dayag Press, 1937). [Written in 1897.]

Khan, Sameera, 'Where Sizzlers and Shakes don't Mix,' *Sunday Times of India* (22 June 1997): 3.

Khare, Randhir, 'The Past is No Burden,' *The Hindu* (Madras, 5 May 1997). [Review of Esther David, *The Walled City* (1997).]

Kirshner, Sheldon, 'Jews of India Practiced a Kind of Apartheid,' *The Canadian Jewish News* (21 June 1990): 12. [Review of Roland (1988).]

Kolabkar, S., *Kolaba Travels Investigations* (Karachi: New Diamond Print Press, 1946).

Kolhatkar, Milind, 'God's Chosen People,' *Poona Digest* (April 1985): 14-17.

Kollet, Shimeon, 'The Bene Israel Tisha B'Ab,' *Kol Bina* 6, 1 (September 1986): 10-12.

Kugel, Seth, 'For One Sect, Curry and Kosher Go Hand in Hand,' *New York Times* (9 December 2001).

Kumar, Anu, 'Ezekiel Fights Poetic Injustice,' *Indian Express* (Mumbai, 4 September 1998): 7. [About poet Nissim Ezekiel.]

Kurulkar, Samuel Shalome, *Gooldhusta* (Bombay, 1878). [A novel in Marathi].

Lehmann, Dr. Manfred R., 'The Bene Israel of Pakistan,' *Jerusalem Post* (14 June 1989): 4. [Letter to the editor.]

———, 'The Karachi Synagogue,' *Brooklyn Jewish Press* (5 February 1993): 88. [Letter to the editor.]

Lentin, Sifra Samuel, 'The Jews of Bombay,' *The Taj Magazine* 24, 4 (1995): 2-21.

———, 'Vintage Mumbai,' *Mid-Day* (9 October 1996): 13.

Levenson, Gabe, 'The Jews of Bombay,' *California B'nai B'rith Messenger* (12 June 1992): 7.

———, 'A Tour of Two Millennia,' *Jewish Week* (13 June 1997): 41.

Lewis, Bea, 'Chanukah Sweets from India,' *Newsday* (4 December 1985): II/9.

Lipman, Steve, 'Jews from India: Minute New York Community Cherishes Unique Hebraic Melodies, Traditions,' *New York Jewish Week* (13 January 1984): 31, 40.

Lipson, Deborah, 'New Life in a New Land: Six Indian Jewish Orphans Immigrate to Israel,' *Brooklyn Jewish Press* (7 October 1994): M11.

Lobo, Melvyn, 'Jewish Synagogues Agog With Activity Again,' *News India* (New York, 23 April 1993): 19.

Lottman, Herbert R., 'The Last Indian Jews,' *Present Tense* 3, 4 (Summer 1976): 7-9.

Mahadevan, Meera Jacob Mendrekar, *Shulamith* (*Apna Ghar*, a novel), (New Delhi: Arnold-Heinemann, 1975 and Delhi: Rajkamal Prakashan, 1961).

Malcioln, José V., *The African Origin of Modern Judaism: From Hebrews to Jews* (Trenton NJ: Africa World Press, 1996): 415-34. [Chapter 12, 'The Bene Israel of India'.]

Masih, Archana, 'For these Jews, Mumbai is the Chosen Land.' *Rediff.com* (11 September 2003) www.rediff.com/cms/print.jsp?docpath=/news/2003/sep/11spec.htm

Mazgaonkar, S.S., 'Bene Israelites in the Indian Army,' *Israelite* 8 (November-December 1924): 153-4.

Menon, Anita, 'A Nissu'in: Anita Menon takes you through the Unique Ritual of a Jewish Wedding,' *Indian Express* (Mumbai, 23 April 2000): 4.

Menon, Kesava, 'Indian Jews Face Identity Crisis in Israel,' *The Hindu* (Madras, 20 November 1997): 4.

Minwalla, Shabnam, 'Mumbai Jews Struggle to Keep the Faith,' *Times of India* (Mumbai, 30 June 2003): 2.

Morris, Leon, 'A Rabbinic Passage to India,' *The Chronicle* 55 (1995): 11-12.

———, 'India's Progressive Synagogue,' *Reform Judaism* 29, no. 2 (Winter 2000): 67.

Moses, Ezra, 'Shaar Hashamaim (Gate of Heaven) Synagogue Appeal,' *Points East* 14, 2 (July 1999): 18.

Moses, Solomon, *The First Bene Israel Conference Report, 1917* (Bombay: The Author, 1918). [In English and Marathi.]

Mukerjee, Sutapa, 'Savant Extraordinaire,' *Free Press Journal* (30 September 1991): 6. (About Elijah Moses Abrahams.]

Mukherjee, Trigunesh, 'Shalom' (magazine article, no data, 1991).

Musleah, Rahel, 'The Jewish Traveler: Bombay,' *Hadassah Magazine* 81, 6 (February 2000): 36-9.

Muthiah, Hepzi, 'Mumbai says Shalom to the Last of the Jewish Policemen,' *The Mumbai Age* (9 January 1997): 9-10.

Nair, Manoj, 'Last of the Rabbis,' *Mid-Day* (Mumbai, 29 July 2000): 4.

———, 'Thane Jews Pass Blood Test,' *Mid-Day* (Mumbai, 23 July 2002).

Nair, Sheeba, 'A Place for Communion, on the Jewish Community Centre which Opened Yesterday at Matunga,' *Times of India* (7 February 1999): 6.

Nair, Shila, 'Shalom Alekhem: Jews of Mumbai, God's Chosen People,' *Afternoon on Sunday* 5, 19 (Bombay, 19 January 1997).

———, 'As Jews in India Celebrate 50 Years of Israel, they still Swear by the Kosher Menu,' *Mumbai Afternoon* (26 April 1998).

Nandgaonkar, Satish, 'Israel Street's Residents Fight On: Artifacts in a 162-year-old Synagogue in Alibaug are Crying for Attention,' *Indian Express* (Mumbai, 31 October 2002), B1, B3.

Nandy, Pritish, 'We Jews Here Are 100 Per Cent Indians,' *Bombay Times* (29 August 2000): 8.

Navgaoker, Solomon Daniel, *Discussion about the Caste System in the Bene Israel Community* (Thana, 1880) [In Marathi.]

Nevins, Ted, 'Gujarat Jews Celebrate Yom Kippur Traditional Way,' *News India-Times* (New York, 29 September 1993): 20. [Reprinted in 'Jewish Worship Services in India,' *Points East* 10, 3 (November 1995): 5-6.]

Newhouse, Alana, 'A Passage from India, Bene Israel-Style,' *Forward* (New York) (15 November 2002): 23. [About Carmit Delman, *Burnt Bread and Chutney.*]

Nissim, Meyer, 'When I was Mayor of Bombay . . .' *India and Israel* 1 (September 1948): 14-15.

Ohr, an occasional bulletin of the Jewish Welfare Association, New Delhi, 1984 - .

Padgaonkar, Dileep, 'Israelis Whose Hearts Belong to India,' *News India* (12 March 1993): 20.

Pais, Arthur, 'Celebrations of Hanukkah with Songs and Oil Lamps,' *India Abroad* (9 January 1987): 1, 14.

Palnitkar, Milind, 'Jews Celebrate Indo-Israel Ties,' *India Abroad* (6 March 1992): 18.

Pande, Alka, 'Esther David: Unwalled!,' *Femina* (1 May 1997): 151-3.

Paranjape, Makarand, 'The first Indian Jewish Novel,' *Outlook* (25 June 1997): 89. [Review of Esther David, *The Walled City.*]

Penkar, Lebana, 'A Tribute to the Indian Jewish Woman,' *Kol India* 14, no. 2 (Mumbai, December 2004): 30.

Perry, John, 'What Happened to Jewish Temples in Pakistan?: Minority Rights Trampled in Pak, Two Jewish Temples Destroyed,' *News India* (18 December 1992): 1, 26.

———, 'What Happened to Jewish Temples in Pakistan?,' *Brooklyn Jewish Press* (1 January 1993): 4.

———, 'Impressive Prayers by Delhi Jews,' *News India* (21 May 1993): 8.

———, 'Indian-Israelis: Indians in the Land of Milk and Honey are Becoming a Prosperous Lot,' *India Worldwide* (January 1995): 4-6.

Pinglay, Daphne Samuel, 'The Bene Israel of Panvel,' *Shalom* (Bombay) (1969-70): 9-11.

Prasad, G.J.V., 'Faith and Foibles,' *Sunday Express* (20 April 1997). [Review of Esther David, *The Walled City* (1997).]

Rabin, Eitan, 'Todah l'Al shehagati l'Eretx HaKodesh,' *Hadashot B'Eretz* (26 December 2004). http://www.nrg.co.il/online/1/

ART/843/581/.html (5 April 2005.) [In Hebrew; about Bene Israel woman from Pakistan.]

Rajpurkar, Joseph Ezekiel, *Scripture Proofs on Jewish Doctrines* (Bombay: Bene Israel Improvement Society, 1876). [In Marathi.]

Ramabai, Pandita, *Wonderful Testimonies—P'La-ot Aydot* (Kedgaon: Mukti Mission Press, 1910/11). [Bible translation in Hebrew, English and Marathi.]

Ranganathan, Murali, 'Bene Israel Documentary Premiere in Washington,' *News India-Times* (1 December 1995): 42.

Rattanaini, Lekha, 'Preserving the Past: A Strikingly Traditional Jewish Community Prepares for Bicentennial Celebrations,' *India Today* (11 August 1995).

Rawal, Samvit, 'Gay Theme Writer Embarks upon Nissim Ezekiel's Biography,' *Maharashtra Herald* (Mumbai, 7 July 1998): 9.

Reuben, Joseph N., *The Co-operative Movement: Considered with Special Reference to the Bene-Israel Community* (Bombay: n.p., 1921).

Reuben, Judge Ezra, *The Housing Problem of the Bene Israels* (Bombay, 1930).

Reuben, Rebecca, *The Bene Israel of Bombay* (Cambridge: Cambridge University Press, Cambridge Jewish Publications no. 4, 1913).

———, *The Bene Israel Annual and Year Book* (Bombay: The Author, 3 vols., vol. I, 1917/18; vol. II, 1918/19; vol. III, 1919/20).

———, 'Religious Reorganization,' *The Bene Israel Annual and Year Book* (Bombay, 1918): III, xviii.

Reubens, D.B., *The Advent and Progress of the Bene-Israels in India* (Ahmedabad: Reubens Educational Trust, n.d. [1990, 1997]).

Reubens, I.D., 'The Jews of Ahmedabad,' in Jacob (1984): 77-8.

———, 'Proud To Be A Jew,' *The Times of India* (Ahmedabad, 18 April 1990): M-10.

———, 'Challenges before Indian Jews,' *Sunday Times of India* (Ahmedabad, 24 September 1995): 12.

Rodrigues, Pradip, 'The Dwindling Jew,' *Sunday Times of India* (Delhi, 13 December 1998): 5.

Ródrigues, Santan, 'Poetic Themes: Nissim Ezekiel's *Collected Poems* Proves His Versatility,' *Sunday* (18-24 June 1989): 75.

Roland, Joan G., 'The Bene Israel in the Konkan in the Eighteenth and Nineteenth Centuries,' *Bulletin of the Jewish Religious Union of India* (March 2004).

Ross, Dan, *Acts of Faith: A Journey to the Fringes of Jewish Identity* (New York: Schocken, 1984): 193-213. [Chapter 10: 'The Bene Israel of Bombay: We Survived'.]

Rothstein, Edward, 'DNA Teaches History a Few Lessons of Its Own,' *New York Times* (24 May 1998): 5. [In part about DNA testing on Bene Israel.]

Rucker, Patricia, 'A New Delhi Chanukah,' *Canadian Jewish News* (23 December 1993): 1, 7.

———, 'The Bene Israel of India: A Unique Story of Jewish Survival,' *Canadian Jewish News* (27 January 1994): 8.

Samson, D.J., 'The Bene-Israel. Why? Where? and Whence?,' in Jacob (1984): 51-4.

Samson, I.J., 'The Religious Beliefs of the Yehudis,' *Israelite* 1 (July 1917): 135-8.

———, 'Marriage and Divorce among the Bene Israel,' *Israelite* 1 (August 1917): 150-2.

———, 'The Communal Economy of the Bene-Israel,' *Israelite* 2 (March 1918): 44-6.

Samuel, Flora, 'Special Food Preparations of the Bene Israel for Festivals,' *Kol Bina* 6, 1 (September 1986): 13-14.

———, *Sanskruti Sangam* (Mumbai: Jai Mulkhar Printing Press, 1996). [A novel in Marathi.]

———, 'The Bene Israel Cradle Ceremony: An Indian Jewish Ritual for the Birth of a Girl,' *Bridges* 7, 1 (1997/8): 43-4.

Samuel, Samuel R., 'The Beni-Israel of India: A Paper Read Before the Central Jewish Literary Society, on the 7th of December, 1904,' *The Jewish Literary Annual* (London: Union of Jewish Literary Societies, 1905): 54-71.

Samuel, Shellim, 'Jews in the Indian Army,' *India and Israel* 4 (February 1952): 21-4.

———, *A Treatise on the Origin and Early History of the Beni-Israel of Maharashtra State* (Bombay: Iyer & Iyer, 1963).

———, 'The Succath Shelomo Synagogue, Poona, on the Occasion of its Golden Jubilee, and the Enlightened and Progressive Jewish Community of Poona,' *Shalom*, special number on the Jews of Poona (Bombay: Indian Zionist Assn., mid-1971): 1-8.

———, 'The Jews of Gujerat,' *Shalom* (Bombay) (1971): 1-11.

———, 'The Bene-Israel: A Short Account of the Origin, History, Contributions and Achievements of the Bene-Israel of India,' in Sophy Kelly, ed., *The Keneseth Eliyahoo Synagogue Centenary Souvenir* (Bombay: Keneseth Eliyahoo Synagogue 1984).

Sankar, Isaac Saul, 'Digging into Ones [*sic*] Roots in India,' *Sharsheret Hadorot: Family Roots Research Periodical* 9, 2 (May 1995): 10-11.

Santos, Emmanuel, 'The Lost Tribes: The Bene Israel of India,' *Generation* (Caulfield South, Victoria, Australia) 47, no. 3 (Autumn 2000): 92-5.

Sartorius, J.A., *Notices of Madras and Cuddalore in the Last Century* from the Journals and Letters of the earlier Missionaries of the Society Promoting Christian Knowledge (London, 1858). [His 1738 reference to 'B'nai Israel' is found on pages 162-4.]

Sassoon, Lynn-Michelle, 'May we have a Bountiful Harvest,' *Bombay Times* (2 October 1996): 5.

Schwartzman, Bryan, 'Judaism's Passage to India Lives On in Queens,' *Brooklyn Jewish Press* (4-10 December 1998): 13.

Sebba, Anne M., 'Vibrant Bombay Jewry using Anniversary to Point Out Community's Contribution to City,' *Jewish Chronicle* (24 November 1995): 6.

Sen, Rehana, 'Shalom Delhi!,' *Indian Express Weekend* (10 September 1988).

Shanson, Lindsey, 'Only one Elderly Jew Remains to Look after Karachi's Jewish Heritage: Synagogue's Legacy is up for Grabs in Legal Battle,' *Jewish Chronicle* (12 March 1993): 8.

Shapurkar, Abraham Samson, *Samuel Ezekiel Hassaji (Samuel Ezekiel Divekar) Commodan. Mukkadam* (Byculla, Bombay: Samuel Yehudah Chincholkar, 1927).

Shedde, Meenakshi, 'Jews in Bombay: Shaky Roots?' *Bombay: The City Magazine* (22 October-6 November 1984): 46-55.

Sheinberg, Rivka, 'A Season of Reflection and Revelry,' *Times of India* (Mumbai, 29 October 1997): 9.

Sheriff, Shameen Akthar, 'Children of Israel,' *The Sunday Times of India* (3 February 1991).

———, 'Notes of a Fading Song,' *Sunday Times of India* (n.d.).

Shirkolkar, Mary, 'For There's No Friend Like a Sister,' *On Being Jewish, Indian and Women* 4 (September 1998): 8-10.

Shivdasani, 'Poet, Lover, Birdwatcher,' *Mumbai Sunday Observer* (13-19 December 1998). [About Nissim Ezekiel.]

Shore, Maj. Irving, 'India's Jews Turn Westward,' *The National Jewish Monthly* 66 (May 1952): 310-11 and 318.

Shulewitz, Malka Hillel, 'The B'nei Israel versus the Rabbinate,' *Jewish Frontier* (October 1963): § 2, 7-11.

Siddiqi, Kamal, 'In Pakistan's City of Strifen 82-year-old Fights for Her Community's Dead,' *Indian Express* (Bombay, 17 December 2000).

Silver, Eric, 'Curried Away: They Built a Successful Chain of Indian Restaurants in Israel—Now they're Taking a Taste of Israel Back to India,' *Jerusalem Report* (23 February 1995): 34.

Sinha, Seema, 'Synagogue Razed during Recent Riots,' *Indian Express* (Bombay, 2 February 1993). [Photo, 30 January 1993.]

Sisterhood of the Jewish Religious Union, *Bene Israel Cook Book* (Bombay: Jewish Religious Union, 1986).

Skarf, Shayna, 'Monsoons, Crowds and "Sea Prayers" The High Holidays in Bombay,' *The Forward* (New York, 29 September 2000): 22, 14.

Solomon, D.J., *Presidential Address to the Seventh Bene Israel Conference* (Bombay: Abraham and Emil, 1924).

Solomon, Dr. Esther, 'Dr. Esther Solomon Looks Back,' *On Being Jewish, Indian and Women* 4 (September 1998): 5-7.

Solomon, Jacob, 'The Mission of the Bene Israelites,' *Israelite* 9 (January-February 1925): 3.

Solomon, Samuel, *Memories, with Thoughts on Gandhi* (London: 1984).

Sommer, Allison Kaplan, 'Indian Jews Fight for Recognition,' *Jerusalem Post International Edition* (6 December 1997): 14.

Staub, Molly Arost, 'Sailing the Asian Sea Change,' *Jewish Sentinel* (New York, 18 and 24 July 1997): 16-17.

Steinsky, Gail, 'A Passage to India,' Brooklyn *Jewish Press* (11 December 1992): 70.

Srinivasan, Shiva Kumar, 'But Where Are the Poets?' *The Express Magazine* (7 May 2000): 3. [Review of R. Raj Rao, *Nissim Ezekiel: The Authorized Biography*, Viking India, 2000).]

Sugbaker, Ilana, 'Memoirs of an Indian Upbringing,' in *The Keys to the Garden: Israeli Writing in the Middle East* (c Farleigh Dickinson University, 1994). No publication data available.

Swenson, Karen, 'Two Synagogues: A Journey in Jewish India,' *Wall Street Journal* (New York, 17 September 1998): A20.

Tarankhopkar, Abraham Salem, 'Bene Israel,' *Friend of Israel* (July-September 1920): 82-5; see also *Israelite* (January-February 1921): 15-16. [In Marathi.]

Thomas, Binu, 'Ancient Faith in Times of Change,' *Sunday Herald Spectrum* 10, 43 (12 September 1999): 1. [About Pune Jewish community.]

Tilak, Shrinivas, 'Jews in India: Indians in Israel, Bene Israel's Search for a Dual Identity,' *Pragati—Montreal* (August-September 1994): 8.

Toker, Elizabeth Ezekiel, 'Karachi Synagogue Dispute,' *Daily News* (Karachi, 15 August 1938).

Torquato, Ronita, 'Relics of Zionism,' *Indian Express Weekend* (20 June 1992).

———, 'Footprints of a Past,' *The Times of India* (6 July 1991): 2.

———, 'For City Jews, India is the "Holy Land"!' (newspaper article; no publication data).

Trivedi, Parag, 'Singing-in the Spring,' *The Times of India* (28 April 1990).

Ullekh, N.P., 'New Sabbath: Delhi's Jewish Community may Soon have a Woman as the Rabbi,' *India Today* (16 September 2003).

Vakrulkar, Solomon M., *Our Synagogues and Their Functions* (Bombay: Abraham Reuben Bhinjekar, 1909).

Von Weisel, Wolfgang, 'The Hindu Jews,' *American Hebrew* (30 August 1929): 405, 409.

Wade, Nicholas, 'Group in Africa Has Jewish Roots, DNA Indicates,' *New York Times* (9 May 1999). [Indicates DNA link of Bene Israel.]

Wajihuddin, Mohammed, 'Nissim, the Moving Force behind Mumbai's Poetry,' *Mumbai Newsline* (12 January 2004). [About Nissim Ezekiel.] <http://cities.expressindia.com fullstory.php?newsid=73040>

Walkar, Simeon Benjamin, *Rebeka Simeon Benjamin Walkar: Reformer, Educationist, Philanthropist*, trans. from Marathi to English by I.A. Isaac (Calcutta, 1925).

Wax, Emily, 'A Mixed Reception: Jews from India find Acceptance, and Skepticism,' *Newsday* (13 January 1999): A31.

Wedler, Marek Alexander, 'Shalom, Bombay,' *Spotlight* (Carol Stream. IL, 31 January 1992): 11.

Weil, Shalva, 'In Memoriam: Flora Samuel,' *Journal of Indo-Judaic Studies* 1, 2 (1999): 150-1.

Weisel, Wolfgang von, 'A 1929 Account of the "Hindu Jews",' *Kulanu* 10, 1 (Silver Spring, MD, 2003): 10.

Weiss, Enid, 'Magazine helps India's 5,000 Jews connect to Judaism,' *The Jewish State* (Highland Park, NJ, 7 August 1998): 1.

———, 'Jewish Life in India has a Long History,' *Jewish Press of Greater Phoenix* (4 September 1998): 3-4. [Reprinted in *Points East* 14, 2 (July 1999): 20.]

Werblowsky, Zwi, 'Bene Israel Battle,' *Jewish Chronicle* (16 March 1962): 1, 40.

Wigoder, Geoffrey, 'Jews in India: A Caste Apart,' *Jerusalem Post International Edition* (17 November 1990). [Review of Roland *Jews in British India* (1989) and Isenberg *India's Bene Israel* (1988).]

Wilson, John, *The Beni-Israel of Bombay: An Appeal for Their Christian Education* (2nd edn., Edinburgh, 1865).

———, 'The Bene-Israel of Bombay,' *The Indian Antiquary* 3 (1874): 321-3.

———, *Lands of the Bible* (Bombay, 1947).

Winkelman, Sara, 'Meeting a Cultural Challenge,' *Wurzweiler Update* (Yeshiva University 10, 2, Fall 1996): 6-7.

———, with Hyam Shafner, 'Our Year among Bombay's Bene Israel,' *Yeshiva University Review* 4, no. 3 (1998/5758): 17-19. [Reprinted in *Points East* 14, 2 (1999): 19.]

Zalizar, Gerry, 'Ha-Derech l'Wakrul (The Road to Wakrul),' *Gesher Quarterly* 35, 2 (1963): 118-21. [In Hebrew.]

Zinkin, Taya, 'The World's Poorest Jews,' *Manchester Guardian* 13 (April 1960).

FILMS, AUDIO CASSETTES

Anonymous, *Bene-Israel Jews of India (Selichot Prayers)* (Jerusalem: Israel Television, n.d.).

———, *Picture a Poet: A Life of Nissim Ezekiel, Indian Jewish Poet* (Bombay: Vireleo Audio Visuals, n.d.).

Hayeem, Benjamin, *Bene Israel—Children of Israel—The Jews of India* (New York, n.d.).

———, *Memories of Jewish India* (New York, n.d.).

Jhirad, Ralphy, and Gidi E. Boss, *Traditional Music of the Bene-Israel, Bombay* (Worli, Mumbai: ORT, 1996). [Analog sound cassette.]

Mehra, Archana, *Professor Nissim Ezekiel: Indian Jewish Poet* (Bombay: Bombay Broadcasting Network, n.d.).

Parzarkar, Reuben, Pinhas David Bhalkar, Benjamin Simon Dandekar, and Levi Jacob, 'Eliyahoo Hanabee: The Musical Tradition of the Bene Israel of Bombay.' CD, no data available.

Spector, Johanna, *About the Jews of India: Shanwar Telis or Bene Israel* (15 mm, 40 mins., Clarksburg, NJ: Alden Films, 1978).

———, *Saturday Oilmen: Bene Israel Jews of India* (London: World ORT Union, n.d.).

Weinshanker, Jack, *Jews of India: Elijah E. Jhirad, President of Congregation BINA of New York* (Linden, NJ: United Synagogue of America, 10/25/89).

CHAPTER 4

Mughal Jews

The Jews who were courtiers of the Mughals and who traded freely throughout the Mughal empire are among the least studied Indian Jewish communities. This is unfortunate, because they are quite fascinating. Their numbers included mystical syncretists (Ezekiel 1974, Hashimi 1934, Schefer 1883, Wali 1924, Katz 1992) as well as advisors to emperors and princes (Lowe 1973). They are not known to have formed a community, although it is reported that Akbar's Court included a synagogue (Fischel 1949).

INCIDENTAL REFERENCES/RELATED SUBJECTS

Edwards, S.M., and H.L.O. Garrertt, *Mughal Rule in India* (Delhi: S. Chand, 1930): 299.

Lowe, W. H., trans., *Muntakhabu-t-Tawârîkh by 'Abdu-l-Qâdir obn-i-Mulûk Shah, known as al-Badâoni*, vol. 2: *The Reign of Akbar from 963 to 1004 A.H.* (Patna: Academica Asiatica, 1973).

Sachau, Edward C., trans., *Alberuni's India: An Account of the Religion, Philosophy, Literature, Geography, Chronology, Astronomy, Customs, Laws and Astrology of India about A.D. 1030* (Delhi: S. Chand, 1964).

Schimmel, Annemarie, *Islam in the Indian Subcontinent* (Leiden-Köln: E.J. Brill, 1980).

STUDIES OF MUGHAL JEWS

Asiri, Fazal Mahmud, trans., *Rubaiyat-i-Sarmad* (Shantiniketan: Vishwa Bharati, 1957).

Azad, Maulana, *Hayat-t-Sarmad* (Lucknow: Tanvir Publishers, n.d.). [In Urdu.]

———, *The Rubaiyat-i-Sarmad* (Delhi: Shahid Kutub Khana, 1963).

Behari, Bankey, *Sufis, Mystics and Yogis of India* (Bombay: Bharatiya Vidya Bhawan, 1962).

Brontá, Robert J. Del, 'Late or Faux Mughal Painting: A Question of Intent,' in Barbara Schmitz, ed., *After the Great Mughals: Painting in Delhi and the Regional Courts in the 18th and 19th Centuries* (Mumbai: Marg Publications, 2002): 150-66. [Painting of Sa'id Sarmad on p. 157.]

Dehlvi, Mohammed Ishaq, ed., *The Rubaiyat-i-Sarmadi* (Delhi: Matha-i-Ahmadi, 1885). [In Urdu.]

Ezekiel, I.A., *Sarmad: Jewish Saint of India* (Punjab: Radha Swami Satsang Beas, 2nd edn. 1974).

Fischel, Walter J., 'Jews and Judaism at the Court of the Moghul Emperors in Medieval India,' *Proceedings of the American Academy for Jewish Research* 18 (1949): 137-77.

———, 'Jews and Judaism at the Court of the Moghul Emperors in Medieval India,' *Islamic Culture* 25 (1951): 105-31.

Gupta, M.G., *Sarmad the Saint* (Agra: M.G. Publishers, 1991).

Hashimi, B.A., 'Sarmad: His Life and Quatrains,' *Islamic Culture* (1933): 663-72, and (1934): 92-104.

Hasrat, Vikram Jit, *Dara Shikoh: Life and Works* (Shantiniketan: Vishwa Bharati, 1953).

Katz, Nathan, 'Sarmad "the Everlasting": An Eccentric Jewish Sufi of Mughal India,' *Journal of the Society of Rabbis in Academia* 2, 1 (January 1992): 13-17.

———, 'Identities and Alliances of Sa'id Sarmad, a Jewish-Yogi-Sufi Courtier of Mughal India,' read at the annual meeting of the American Academy of Religion, New Orleans, LA, 24 November 1996.

———, 'The Identity of a Mystic: The Case of Sa'id Sarmad, a Jewish-Yogi-Sufi Courtier of the Mughals,' *Numen* 47 (Leiden, Netherlands, 2000): 142-60.

———, 'The Identity of a Mystic: The Case of Sa'id Sarmad, a Jewish-Yogi-Sufi Courtier of the Mughals,' *Journal of Indo-Judaic Studies* 7-8 (2004-5): 84-99.

Krishnan, Lajwanti Ram, *Punjabi Sufi Poets, 1460-1900* (Calcutta: Oxford University Press, 1950).

Marghoob, Munshi Fazl-i-Ilahi, ed., *The Rubaiyat-i-Sarmad* (Lahore: Marghoob Book Agency, 1920). [In Urdu.]

Mohammad, Aqa Mirza, ed., *The Rubaiyat-i-Shah Sarmad Sarmast* (Bombay: CP Press, 1892).

Qanugo, K.R., *Dara Shikoh, Part I* (Calcutta: M.C. Sarkar & Sons, 1935).

Rai, Lakhpat, *Sarmad: His Life and Rubais* (Gorakhpur: Hanuman Prasad Poddar Smarak Samiti, 1978).

Sarmadi, Sayeed Mohammed Ahmad, *Tazikira Hazrat Sarmad Shaheed* (Biography of Revered Martyr Sarmad) (Delhi, 1910; rpt. Delhi: Kitab Khana-e-Sarmadi, n.d.). [In Urdu.] [Hindi trans. by Ahmed Jalees.]

Schefer, Charles, 'Notice sur le Kitab Beïan il Edian (Exposé des Religions),' *Publication des Langues Orientales Vivantes*, 2nd ser, 7 (1883): 132-81. [Persian text of Sarmad's *Ruba'iyat*.]

Sharma, S.R., *Religious Policy of the Mughal Emperors* (Calcutta: Oxford University Press, 1940).

Shea, David, and Anthony Troyer, trans., *The Dabistan, or School of Manners* (Washington and London: M. Walter Dunne Publ., 1901). [See esp. 'The Yahuds (Jews)': 299-312.]

Sikand, Yoginder, 'Sarmad Shahid, the "Martyr for Love",' in *Sacred Spaces: Exploring Traditions of Shared Faith in India* (New Delhi: Penguin, 2003).

Wali, Maulavi 'Abdul, 'A Sketch of the Life of Sarmad,' *Journal of the Asiatic Society of Bengal* 20 (1924): 111-22.

CHAPTER 5

The Baghdadi (and Sephardi) Jews

PRIMARY DOCUMENTS/MEMOIRS

Primary sources about 'Baghdadi' Jews in India—Jews from Iraq, Syria, Afghanistan and Iran who arrived at the end of the eighteenth and early during the nineteenth centuries—include local publications, synagogue souvenirs, and a few liturgical collections.

Abraham, C.S., *A Story of Calcutta* (London: C.S. Benjamin & Co., 1925). [A novel.]

Alkalai, Judah, *Kol kore: 'im sharh 'Aravi* (Bombay: Ba-defus ha-meshubah ha-hadash shel Yekezkel Shem Tov David, 1887). [In Hebrew.]

Anonymous, 'How the Rangoon Synagogue was Saved,' *Sephardi Bulletin* (Sydney, Australia: New South Wales Association of Sephardim, 1945).

Ben Yaacov, Avraham, 'Diary of the First Jewish Settler in Calcutta, Shalom ben Ovadia Hacohen from Aleppo,' *Sefunot* (Jerusalem: Ben Zvi Institute, 1964). [In Hebrew.]

Cohen, Rev. E.M.D., 'Judaism (3rd Paper),' in *Convention of Religions in India (Report of the First Convention of Religions in India 1909)* (Delhi: Bimla Publishing House, 1982 [1909]): 59-68.

Cohen, Israel, *The Journal of a Jewish Traveller* (New York, Dodd: Mead and Co., 1925).

Dabar Be-'Itto, series of booklets published during World War I by the Supervising Officer for Jewish Soldiers in India, Queen's Barracks, Ft. William, Calcutta.

David, Yohanan ben (Samson John David), *These Days Will Never Come Back* (New Delhi: Northern Book Centre, 2002).

Hyman, Mavis, *Jews of the Raj* (London: Hyman Publishers, 1995).

Isaac, I.A., *Letters and Speeches* (Calcutta: Telegraph Association Press, 1917).

Jacob, Lt. Gen. J.F.R., *Surrender at Dacca: Birth of a Nation* (New Delhi: Manohar, 1999).

Jewish Tribune Devoted to the Welfare of Indian Jewry, The (Bombay: The Organ, 1933). [One issue known to have been published, March 1933.]

Kelly, Sophy, ed., *The Keneseth Eliyahoo Synagogue Centenary Souvenir* (Bombay: Keneseth Eliyahoo, 1985).

Kywe, U Aung, and Moses Samuels, *Musmeah Yeshua Synagogue and Jewish Community in Myanmar* (Yangon: Musmeah Yeshua Synagogue, 1991).

Maggid Mesharim, Hebrew weekly, publ. Hakham Sholomo (Calcutta: 7 November 1889-2 October 1900).

Mebasser: Union of Orthodox Jewish Congregations of India, vol. 1, no. 13 (15 April 1961). [Copy in N.Y. Public Library; other issues unknown.]

Musleah, Rabbi Ezekiel N., *Order of Service, on the occasion of the Seventy-Fifth Anniversary of the Dedication of the Maghen David Synagogue, incorporating a Brief History of the Synagogue and a Biographical Sketch of the Late Rev. E.M.D. Cohen* (Calcutta: Maghen David Synagogue, 1960).

———, ed. & trans., *Kol Zimra: The Sound of Song* (Brooklyn: Israel Shelanu, 1983).

———, *No Short Cuts to Far Horizons: Pioneering Paths from Jewish India* (Philadelphia: privately published, 2003).

Musleah, Rahel, *Songs of the Jews of Calcutta* (Cedarhurst, NY: Tara Publications, 1991). [Book and cassette.]

Pairah, 4-page Hebrew weekly, ed. Moses Mayohas and Elias Solomon (1978), Moses Mayohas (1878-81), Rev. E.M.D. Cohen (1881-89) (Calcutta: 21 June 1878-27 February 1889).

Samuels, Jacob, *Appeal to Brethren Near and Far* (Rangoon: Musmeah Yeshua Synagogue, 1980).

Samuels, Moses and U Aung Kywe, *Musmeah Yeshua Synagogue and Jewish Community in Burma* (Rangoon: Musmeah Yeshua Synagogue, 1980).

Saul, Geoffrey, 'The Road to Mandalay: A History of the Sassoon, Salomon and Saul Families — Jewish Pioneers in Colonial Burma.' Unpublished manuscript.

Saul, Solly, 'Memories of Burma,' *Sephardi Bulletin* (Sydney, Australia: New South Wales Association of Sephardim, 1995).

Solomon, Sally, *Hooghly Tales: Stories of growing up in Calcutta under the Raj* (London: David Ashley, 1998).

INCIDENTAL REFERENCES/RELATED SUBJECTS

Baghdadi Jews were instrumental in the development of Bombay and in the commercial life of Calcutta and Rangoon. Their best known family was the Sassoons, known as 'the Rothschilds of the East' (Jackson 1968, Roth 1977), although the Ezras and Eliases of Calcutta were nearly their equals in wealth and prestige. Some other intriguing Baghdadi personalities of Calcutta are the community's founder, Shalom Obaidah Hacohen and Rev. E.M.D. Cohen, the community's nineteenth-century spiritual leader.

An intriguing chapter in their history, and one which has not been satisfactorily documented, is their role in the rescue of Jews fleeing Nazi-dominated Europe. Brief references to this noble chapter in Indian Jewish history is found in discussions of Japan's ambivalent role in World War II and the refuge Jews found in Shanghai (Tokayer and Swarz 1979, Kranzler 1976).

Jackson, Stanley, *The Sassoons* (New York: Dutton, 1968).

Khan, Aisha, '25 Years After the Bangladesh War,' *Asian Age* (16 December 1996): 13. [Interview with Gen. J.F.R. Jacob.]

Klein-Halevi, Yossi, 'Defending Mother Rachel,' *Jerusalem Report* (24 August 1995): 18-19.

Kranzler, David, *Japanese, Nazis and Jews* (New York: Yeshiva University Press, 1976).

Leitner, Yecheskel, *Operation Torah Rescue: The Escape of the Mirrer Yeshiva from War-torn Poland to Shanghai, China* (Jerusalem and New York: Feldheim Publishers, 1987).

Roth, Cecil, *The Sassoon Dynasty* (New York: Arno Press, 1977 [London: Robert Hale Ltd., 1941]).

Tokayer, Marvin, and Mary Swartz, *The Fugu Plan: The Untold Story of the Japanese and the Jews during World War II* (New York and London: Paddington Press, 1979).

SCHOLARLY STUDIES OF BAGHDADI JEWS

Musleah (1975) and Ezra (1986), both formerly of Calcutta, wrote outstanding histories of the Calcutta Baghdadi community. Unfortunately, no comparable work has been done about Bombay, much less Rangoon. Fischel (1964, 1965, 1972), Timberg (1974 and two 1986 articles), Roland (1999, 2002, 2003) and Cernea (1995) have paid attention to these fabled communities.

Ben-Jacob, Abraham, 'The Diary of the First Jewish Settler in Calcutta, R. Shalom Ovadia Hacohen of Aleppo,' in Meir Benyahu, ed., *Itzhak Ben-Zvi Memorial Volume: Studies and Texts on the History of the Jewish Communities in the East*, vol. 2 (Jerusalem: Ben-Zvi Institute in the Hebrew University, 1964): 361-82. [In Hebrew.]

———, *Yehude Bavel ba-tesutsot* (Yerushalayim: R. Mas, 1985). [In Hebrew.]

———, 'Hagirat Yehude Bavel le-Hodu ve-hishtak'utam bah: ba-aspaklaryah shel ha-'itonuit ha-mekomit be-'Arvit-Yehudit u-mekorot aherim,' Ph.D. dissertation, Hebrew University, 1986. [In Hebrew.]

Betta, Chiara, 'The Trade Diaspora of Baghdadi Jews: From India to China's Treaty Ports, 1842-1937,' in Ina Baghdiantz, Gelina Harlaftis, and Ionna Pepelasis Minoglou, eds., *Diaspora Entrepreneurial Networks: Four Centuries of History* (Oxford, U.K. and New York: Berg, 2005): 269-85.

———, ed., *Identities of Baghdadi Jews of the Jewish Diaspora: India, Singapore, Hong Kong, and Shanghai* (Palo Alto CA: Sino-Judaic Institute, *Sino Judaica: Occasional Papers of the Sino-Judaic Institute*, vol. 4, 2003).

Biedler, Joan, 'Jewish Identity in Singapore: Cohesion, Dispersion, Survival,' in Chiara Betta, ed., *Identities of Baghdadi Jews of the Jewish Diaspora: India, Singapore, Hong Kong, and Shanghai* (Palo Alto CA: Sino-Judaic Institute, *Sino Judaica: Occasional Papers of the Sino-Judaic Institute*, vol. 4, 2003): 29-58.

Cernea, Ruth Fredman, 'The Conditions of Jewish Identity in Burma,' a paper read at the annual meeting of the American Academy of Religion, New Orleans, LA, 19 November 1990.

———, 'Promised Lands and Domestic Arguments: The Conditions of Jewish Identity in Burma,' in Nathan Katz, ed., *Studies of Indian-Jewish Identity* (New Delhi: Manohar, 1995): 153-72.

Cooper, John and Judy, 'The Life-cycle of the Baghdadi Jews of India,' in Shalva Weil, ed., *India's Jewish Heritage: Ritual, Art, & Life-Cycle* (Mumbai: Marg Publications, 2002): 101-9.

Ezra, Esmond David, *Jewish Graves in Calcutta: A Supplementary List* (London, 1984).

———, *Turning Back the Pages: A Chronicle of Calcutta Jewry*, 2 vols. (London: Brookside Press, 1986).

———, 'The Founder of the Jewish Community of Calcutta,' *Kol Bina* 7, 1 (April 1989): 7-9.

Fischel, Walter J., 'Leading Jews in the Service of Portuguese India,' *Jewish Quarterly Review* (Philadelphia) 47 (July 1956), pp. 37-57.

———, 'The Activities of a Jewish Merchant House in Bengal (1786-98),' *Révue des Études Juives* 3, 4 (1964): 433-98.

———, 'Pedro Pereira: The Jewish Merchant in Surat, 1636-1721,' *Sefunot* (Jerusalem, Ben Zvi Institute, 1964). [In Hebrew.]

———, 'The Immigration of "Arabian Jews" to India in the Eighteenth Century,' *Proceedings of the American Academy for Jewish Research* 33 (1965): 1-20.

———, 'Bombay in Jewish History in the Light of New Documents from the Indian Archives,' *Proceedings of the American Academy for Jewish Research* 38, 9 (1972): 119-44.

Goldstein, Jonathan, 'The Sorkin and Golab Theses and their Applicability to South, Southeast, and East Asian Port Jews,' *Jewish History and Culture* (London) 4, 2 (Winter 2001): 179-96. [Republished in David Cesarani (ed.), *Port Jews: Jewish Communities in Cosmopolitan Maritime Trading Centers, 1550-1950* (London: Frank Cass, 2002, pp. 179-96).]

Johnson, Barbara C., 'Baghdadi Jews of India,' in Michael Terry, ed., *Reader's Guide to Judaism* (Chicago: Dearborn, 2000): 62-3.

———, 'Review of Jael Silliman, *Jewish Portraits, Indian Frames: Women's Narratives from a Diaspora of Hope* (2001),' *Journal of Indo-Judaic Studies* (Saskatoon) 6 (2003): 103-6.

Lentin, Sifra Samuel, 'The Jewish Presence in Bombay,' in Shalva Weil, ed., *India's Jewish Heritage: Ritual, Art, & Life-Cycle* (Mumbai: Marg Publications, 2002): 23-35.

Manasseh, Sara, 'Variation and Stability in *Shaboth*: Songs of Praise of the Babylonian Jews,' in A. Buckley, K-O Edstrom and P. Nixon, eds., *Proceedings of the Second British-Swedish Conference on Musicology: Ethnomusicology,* Cambridge, 5-10 August 1989 (Skrifter från Musikvetenskapliga institutionen, Göteborgs universitet, nr 26, 1991): 231-51.

———, 'Aspects of Babylonian Jewish Life in Iraq and India during the 19th and 20th Centuries,' *The Jewish Babylonian* (New York: Midrash Ben Ish Hai): Part I: 2-3 (Winter 1998); Part II: 4-5 (Winter 1999); Part III: 2-3 (Summer 2000).

———, 'Religious Music Traditions of the Jewish Babylonian Diaspora of Bombay,' in Margaret J. Kartom and Andrew D. McCredie, eds., *Musical Outcomes of Jewish Diasporas in East and Southeast Asia*. [Publication data unavailable.]

Masliyah, Sadok, 'The Bene Israel and the Baghdadis: Two Indian Jewish Communities in Conflict,' *Judaism* 43/3 (Summer 1994): 279-93.

Musleah, Rabbi Ezekiel N., *On the Banks of the Ganga: The Sojourn of Jews in Calcutta* (North Quincy, MA: Christopher Publishing House, 1975).

Musleah, Rahel, *Songs of the Jews of Calcutta* (Cedarhurst, NY: Tara Publications, 1991). [Book and cassette.]

Plüss, Carolina, 'Globalizing Ethnicity with Multi-Local Identifications: The Parsee, Indian Muslim and Sephardic Trade Diasporas in Hong Kong,' in Ina Baghdiantz, Gelina Harlaftis, and Ionna Pepelasis Minoglou, eds., *Diaspora Entrepreneurial Networks: Four Centuries of History* (Oxford, U.K., and New York: Berg, 2005): 245-68.

Ristaino, Marcia R., 'Reflections on the Sephardi Trade Diaspora in South, Southeast and East Asia,' in Chiara Betta, ed., *Identities of Baghdadi Jews of the Jewish Diaspora: India, Singapore, Hong Kong, and Shanghai* (Palo Alto CA: Sino-Judaic Institute, *Sino Judaica: Occasional Papers of the Sino-Judaic Institute*, vol. 4, 2003): 105-24.

Roland, Joan G., 'Baghdadi Jews in India,' *Jews of India* (Jerusalem, Jewish Museum, 1995): 37-44. [Exhibition catalogue.]

———, 'Baghdadi Jews in India and China in the Nineteenth Century: A Comparison of Economic Roles,' in Jonathan Goldstein, ed., *The Jews of China*, vol. I, *Historical and Comparative Perspectives* (Armonk NY: M.E. Sharpe, 1999): 141-56.

———, 'The Baghdadi Jews of India: Perspectives on the Study and Portrayal of a Community,' Read at 'A View from the Margin: The State of the Art of Indo-Judaic Studies,' Oxford Centre for Hebrew and Jewish Studies, U.K., 2-6 July 2002.

———, 'Baghdadi Jews in India: Communal Relationships, Nationalism, Zionism and the Construction of Identity,' in Chiara Betta, ed., *Identities of Baghdadi Jews of the Jewish Diaspora: India, Singapore, Hong Kong, and Shanghai* (Palo Alto CA: Sino-Judaic Institute, *Sino Judaica: Occasional Papers of the Sino-Judaic Institute*, vol. 4, 2003): 1-28.

———, 'Crossing Borders, Maintaining Boundaries: The Life and Times of Farha, a Woman of the Baghdadi Jewish Diaspora (1870-1958),' *Journal of Indo-Judaic Studies* (Saskatoon) 1, 1 (1998): 57-79.

———, *Jewish Portraits, Indian Frames: Women's Narratives from a Diaspora of Hope* (Hanover and London: University Press of New England, and Calcutta: Seagull Books, 2001).

Timberg, Thomas A., 'The Jews of Calcutta,' *Bengal Past and Present* 93, 1, 175 (1974): 7-22.

———, 'The Jews of Calcutta,' in Thomas A. Timberg, ed., *Jews in India* (New Delhi: Vikas, 1986): 28-34.

———, 'Baghdadi Jews in Indian Port Cities,' in Thomas A. Timberg, ed., *Jews in India* (New Delhi: Vikas, 1986): 273-84.

———, 'Iraqi Jews: What Marginality? Or Rather, From Roots to Marginality.' Paper read at the annual meeting of the American Academy of Religion, New Orleans, LA, 19 November 1990.

———, 'Indigenous and Non-Indigenous Jews,' in Nathan Katz, ed., *Studies of Indian-Jewish Identity* (New Delhi: Manohar, 1995): 135-52.

———, 'Review of Dalia Roy, *The Jewish Heritage of Calcutta* (2001),' *Journal of Indo-Judaic Studies* (Saskatoon) 6 (2003): 107-9.

Weil, Shalva, 'Review of M. Hyman *The Jews of the Raj* (1995),' *Journal of Indo-Judaic Studies* 1, 1 (1998): 105-7.

Weinstein, Brian, 'Judaeo-Arabic in India,' *Journal of Indo-Judaic Studies* 2 (1999): 53-68.

———, 'Charity and Public Service of the Babylonian Jews in India,' in Yitzhak Avishur and Zvi Yehuda (eds.), *Studies in the History and Culture of the Jews in Babylonia: Proceedings of the Second International Congress for Babylonian Jewry Research (June 1998)* (Israel: The Babylonian Jewry Heritage Center, 2002): 231-46.

Weinstein, Judah, 'Yehudai-Bavel b'Hodu,' *Shluchot* 26 (Iyar-Sivan, 1951): 17-19. [In Hebrew.]

Wexler, Paul, 'Notes on the Iraqi Judaeo-Arabic of Eastern Asia,' *Journal of Semitic Studies* 28, 2 (1983): 337-54.

Yegar, Moshe, 'L'Toldot HaKehilah HaYehudim B'Singapore' (History of the Jewish Community in Singapore), *Gesher* 78 (1974): 50-65). [In Hebrew.]

———, 'The Jewish Community in Penang Malaysia,' *Sephardi World* 4-5 (October-January 1984): 42-3.

GENERAL & NEWSPAPER ACCOUNTS OF BAGHDADI JEWS

Memoirs and histories by Calcutta Jews include Isaac (1917), Abraham (1969) and Elias and Cooper (1974). Meyer (1949) offers the only indigenous study of the Rangoon community, and Cowen (1969, 1973) provides a charming account of a Sukkot custom.

Abraham, Isaac S., *The Origin and History of the Calcutta Jews* (Calcutta: Daw Sen & Co., 1969).

Ahmed, Ashmee Z., '*Calcutta Kosher* and the Jewish Question,' *Times of India* (New Delhi, 21 February 2004). http://timesofindia.com/articleshow/511007.cms

Anonymous, 'Zail to Open Synagogue Fete' and 'Zail Lauds Jews,' *Indian Express* (no publication data available).

———, 'East Meets West at Sephardic Congregation of Long Beach,' *Brooklyn Jewish Press* (20 April 1990): M30-M31.

———, 'Landmark Decision to Save Synagogue,' *News India* (New York, 7 August 1992): 11.

———, 'Pune has World's Largest Synagogue,' *Asian Age* (31 August 1995).

———, 'Last Jews of Burma Want some Promise from Their Land,' *Asian Age* (27 November 1995): 1. [Reprinted as 'Burmese Jews Seek Some Promise From Their Land,' *News India-Times* (12 January 1996):12.]

———, 'Sassoon Library: No Place for Landsharks,' *Bombay Times* (31 January 1996): 2.

———, 'Jewish Tombs not to be Moved: Burma Agrees not to

Relocate Cemetery,' *The Asian Age* (4 February 1997): 7.

———, 'Shadows on the Horizon for Dwindling Flock,' *Points East* 12, 2 (July 1997): 6. [Reprinted from *South China Morning Post* (5 January 1997)].

———, 'Rangoon to Halt Relocation of 700 Jewish Graves: Israeli Ambassador,' *Points East* 12, 2 (July 1997): 7. [Reprinted from *Agence France-Presse* (4 February 1997)].

———, 'D'Souza Installed as Goa Chief Minister,' *News India-Times* (28, no. 32 New York, 7 August 1998): 1, 16. [Also about J.F.R. Jacob, Governor of Goa.]

———, 'Jews in Buddhist Myanmar Live Freely. But for How Long?' *The Internet Jerusalem Post* (27 May 2001). http://cgis.jpost.com/cgi-bin/General/printarticle.cgi?article=/Editions/2001/05/

Arbell, Mordechai, 'The Portuguese Jewish Community of Madras, India, in the Seventeenth Century,' (2000) www.sefarad.org/publication/lm/041/5.html.

Balaram, Gunvanthi 'David Sassoon Library Opens Its Doors to Art,' *Times of India* (18 August 1997): 5.

Barber, Ben, 'Handful of Jews Linger on in India after a New Exodus,' *Los Angeles Herald* (4 May 1983).

Berzilai, Amnon, 'The Jewish General Who Beat Pakistan,' *Haaretz.com* (22 September 2004). www.haaretz.com/hasen/spages/474003.html

Beyer, Shula, 'Oh, Calcutta! On Friday Night, Far from Home, There's no Place Like Nahoum's,' *Moment* (October 1984): 43-5.

Bhattacharyya, Sourish, 'Shooting from The Nip,' *Express Magazine* (Mumbai, 27 April 1997)]: 1. [About J.F.R. Jacob.]

Bose, Derek, 'The Vanishing Glory,' *Deccan Herald* (18 August 1996).

Cembalest, Robin, 'Treasure of a Wandering Jew: From India to Amsterdam, Sotheby's Auctions Judaica Gems,' *Forward* (17 June 1994): 8.

Cernea, Ruth Fredman, 'End of the Road: The Last Burmese Jews,' *Jewish Monthly* (June-July 1988): 26-30.

———, 'The Last Burmese Jews,' *Points East* 4, 1 (February 1989): 12-13.

———, 'Golden Age in Rangoon,' *Moment Magazine* (February 1999): 33-5.

Chowdhury, Srinjoy, 'Patriot Games,' *The Telegraph* (27 April 1997): 14. [About J.F.R. Jacob.]

Christy, Rajnid N., 'The Cared for . . . and the Neglected,' *Madras Musings* (16-30 September 1993): 6. [About Madras Jewish cemetery.]

Colvin, John, *Lions of Judah* (London: Quartet Books, 1997). [Chapter 43, 'India,' pp. 260-5, is about Lt. Gen. Frederick Jacob.]

Corley, Rizpah, 'Jews Around the World: Burma,' *Kol India* 8, 1 (Mumbai, December 1998): 16.

Courter, Gay, *Flowers in the Blood* (New York: E.P. Dutton, 1990). [A novel.]

Cowen, Ida G., 'Calcutta's Sukkot Queen of Beauty,' *The Reconstructionist* 35, 10 (10 October 1969): 20-1 & 24-5.

———, 'Calcutta's Sukkot Queen of Beauty,' in Philip Goodman, ed., *The Sukkot and Simhat Torah Anthology* (Philadelphia: Jewish Publication Society, 1973): 233-5.

Crosette, Barbara, 'Rightist Party in India Gets Wide Backing,' *New York Times* (8 May 1991): A15. [Mentions Gen. J.F.R. Jacob.]

Das Gupta, Prosenjit, 'Heritage Trail/ Maghan David Synagogue: The Bearer of Glorious Memories,' *Hindustan Times* (30 November 2003).

Elias, Flower, and Judith Elias Cooper, *The Jews of Calcutta: The Autobiography of a Community 1798-1972* (Calcutta: The Jewish Association of Calcutta, 1974).

Fishkoff, Sue, 'Burmese Jews Hang on Despite Dire Predictions,' *Jerusalem Post International Edition* (28 August 1993): 8B. [Reprinted in *Points East* 8, 1 (April 1994): 11-12.]

Goodman, Matthew, 'In India, a Community Blooms, Then Withers,' *Forward* (26 October 2001): 17. [About Baghdadi cuisine.]

Gordon, Buzzy, 'The Jews of Singapore,' *Jerusalem Post Internet Edition* (2 July 1999/18 Tammuz 5759).

Gourgey, Percy Sassoon, 'Iraqi Jews in India in the Twentieth Century,' *Journal of the Babylonian Jewry Heritage Center* 6 (March 1993): 8.

Isaac, I.A., *A Short Account of the Calcutta Jews, with a Sketch of the Bene-Israels, the Cochin Jews, the Chinese Jews and the Black Jews of Abyssinia* (Calcutta: The Author, 1917).

———, 'Leading Features of Israelitism (Judaism),' in *Convention of Religions in India (Report of the First Convention of Religions in India 1909)* (Delhi: Bimla Publishing House, 1982 [1909]): 45-52.

Ivy, Daisy, *The Best of Baghdad Cooking* (New York: Saturday Review Press/E.P. Dutton, 1976).

Kamm, Henry, 'Burma's Last Few Jews Living on Proud Memories,' *New York Times* (10 August 1980): 6.

Kay, Marcia, 'Chef Plans Indian Holiday Feast,' *Washington Jewish Week* (25 August 1994): 1, 8.

———, 'An Indian Holiday Feast,' *Points East* 9, 3 (November 1994): 15-16. [Reprint of above.]

Kirshner, Sheldon, 'Jewish General Led Indian Army in 1971 War,' *World Affairs Board* (26 September 2005).

Krausz, Tibor, 'Our Rebbe's a Buddhist,' *Jerusalem Report* (3 July 2000): 34-5.

Manasseh, Rachel and Sara, 'The Baghdadian Jews of India,' *The Scribe: Journal of Babylonian Jewry* 61 (May 1994): 12-13, and 62 (September 1994): 32-3.

Marks, Copeland, 'Calcutta's Sephardic Cooking,' *The Pleasures of Cooking* 8, 3 (November/December 1985): 13-17.

———, 'The Jewish Kitchen (Cooking of the Jews of Calcutta),' in *The Varied Kitchens of India* (New York: M. Evans & Co., 1986).

Mayer, Jean-François, 'Birmanie (Myanmar): Il Ne reste Que Vingt Juifs,' *Relgiioscope* (23 July 2002). <www.religioscope.com/notes/2002/041_jews_burma.htm> [In French.]

Mehta, Ashok K., 'A Rethinking on the 1971 War with Pakistan,'

India Abroad (4 July 1997): 2. [About Gen. J.F.R. Jacob.]

Meyer, Nissim A., 'The Jewish Community of Rangoon,' *Shema* 3, 8 (January 1949): 7, 15.

Mitra, Rathin, 'India: A Haven Away from Home for the Jews,' *Asian Age* (20 April 1995): 24.

Musleah, Rahel, 'The High Holy Days, Calcutta Style,' *NY Jewish Sentinel* (20-25 September 1996): 12.

———, 'Bazaar of Generations,' *Hadassah Magazine* 79, 3 (November 1997): 22-6.

———, 'The Jewish Traveler: Calcutta,' *Hadassah Magazine* 79, 3 (November 1997): 28-31.

Mydans, Seth, 'Burmese Jew Shoulders Burden of His Heritage,' *New York Times* (23 July 2002).

Oberdorfer, Don, 'Abraham Sofaer: Sate's Legal Adviser Deals With Policy, Then the Law,' *Washington Post Federal Report* (10 March 1986): A13.

Patel, Kusum S., 'Review of Gay Courter,' *Indo-American Library of New England Newsletter* 2, 2 (1995): 4.

Patel, Tara, 'Madame Sophy Kelly: A Teacher for all Seasons,' *Mumbai Afternoon* (26 April 1998): 16-17.

Preschel, Tovia, 'Profile: The Sassoon Manuscripts Sotheby's London Auction,' *Brooklyn Jewish Press* (17 June 1994): 54; (24 June 1994): 59.

———, 'Jerusalem's India-Born Kabbalist Rabbi Ya'akov Moshe Hillel,' *Brooklyn Jewish Press* (11 August 1995): 13.

———, 'Profile: A Few Words About The Sassoons, "The Rothschilds of the East",' *Brooklyn Jewish Press* (23 April 1999): 63; (7 May 1999): 33, 45; (14 May 1999): 101; (21 May 1999): 89; (28 May 1999): 68; (4 June 1999): 83.

Rabin, Keith W., 'In Burma, Getting a Minyan Together, Even on Yom Kippur, Is Not Easy,' *The Jewish Week-American Examiner* (11 July 1982): 29-30.

Reichek, Mort, 'Hospitable Calcutta Jews Served Chopped Liver,' *Forward* (26 October 2001): 12. [Letter to the editor.]

Robbins, Kenneth X, 'The Jewish Community of Calcutta,'

Highlights: Notes, News and Views on Arts, History and Letters of India 1, 1 & 2 (1991): 41-50.

———, 'The Jewish Community of Calcutta,' in Raj Krishna, ed., *From Thames to Hooghly: Calcutta Heritage, 1890-1990* (New Delhi: Veerendra, 1991).

———, 'The Jewish Community of Calcutta,' *Points East* 8, 1 (February 1993): 6-9.

———, 'Merchants and Traders,' *Traveler's India* 2, 3 (1998): 17.

Roland, Joan G., 'Baghdadi Jews in India: Communal Relationships, Nationalism and Zionism and the Construction of Identity,' *Sino-Judaica* 4 (2003).

Rosenberg, Barbara Ann, 'An Indian Rosh Hashanah: The Foreign Flavors & Heartfelt Feelings of a Calcutta Feast,' *Washington Post* (16 September 1987).

———, 'Yom Kippur in India at Miss Kelly's Home,' *Philadelphia Inquirer* (23 September 1990).

Rustam, 'Haskell David Will Stay,' *The Metropolitan* (Calcutta, 19 December 1987).

Sargon, Joseph I., 'Baghdadi Jews of India and the Sassoons,' *Jewish Daily* (25 August 1987).

Sassoon, David S.D., 'Jewish Travellers in Bombay,' *The Jewish Tribune* (Bombay) (September 1933): 17, 40-1 (October 1933): 10-11.

Saul, Solly, 'Memories of Burma,' *Sephardi Bulletin* (Nissan 5755/ March 1995): 14-15.

Shulman, H., 'Burma Native Realizes Dream of Attending YU,' *Yeshiva University Today Online* 8, no. 4 (New York, Fall 2002). www.yu.edu/news/yutoday/fall02/burma.html

Shedde, Meenakshi, 'When the Newspaper Snored,' *Times of India* (7 December 1996): 3. [About the David Sassoon Library.]

Sinai, Annie, 'Once There Was a Burmese Jewry,' *Women's League Outlook* (Spring 1969): 12-13, 26, 28.

Solomon, Sally Luddy, 'Coming of Age in Calcutta,' *Inside* (Winter 1986): 70-1, 119-21.

———, 'Potato Pursuit: Fridays in Calcutta were Devoted to

Shopping for and Preparing a Special Sabbath Dinner,' *Inside* (Summer 1991): 42ff.

———, 'Babylonian Jewry in the Diaspora: Feasting and Fasting,' *Nehardea* 9 (December 1996): 12-13.

Solomon, Sally, 'Moving Stones,' *Shemot* 3, 2 (n.d.): 13, 18. [About Jews of Madras.]

Suri, Sanjay, 'The Echoes of Jewish Music,' *India Abroad* (15 April 1994): 46.

Tharoor, Shashi, 'Research and Anecdote,' *The Hindu* (Madras) (23 June 2002). [About Jael Silliman, *Jewish Portraits, Jewish Frames*, 2001].

Whiting, Dominic, 'The Burma Road to Israel,' *Jerusalem Post International Edition* (31 May 2002): 28.

Yeger, Moshe, 'A Rapid and Recent Rise and Fall,' *Sephardi World* (July-August 1984).

Yehudi, Prem Doss Swami Doss, 'Indian Jews & Opium Trade,' *New Swatantra Times* (no publication data). [Review of Courter.]

FILMS & AUDIOCASSETTES/CDs

Anonymous, *The Jewish Wedding in Baghdad* (Yehuda, Israel: Babylonian Jewish Heritage Center, n.d.).

———, *David Sassoon: The Great Philanthropist* (Bombay: ORT India, 1996?).

Benjamin, Hayeen, *Memories of Jewish India* (New York: Angelika Films, 1993/1985) Videorecording, American Sephardi Federation.

Frisch, Larry, *The Last Jews In Calcutta,* with Albert Jacob (NJ, RBIS, n.d.).

Musleah, Rahel, 'Hodu: Jewish Rhythms From Baghdad (Iraq) to India,' CD, no data available.

Natan, Abe, *'Im Ebi Natan* (Yerushalayim: Kol Yisra'el, 1992/80). Recording of radio programme.

CHAPTER 6

Ashkenazim in India

There has always been a trickle of European Jews who found their way to India, sometimes in search of riches, sometimes of enlightenment. Often, they merged into local communities in Bombay or Cochin. On occasion, they became freelance mystics—such as the Kabbalist who was the ritual slaughterer in Darjeeling. During the World War II era, thousands of Ashkenazim—many of them physicians—found refuge in India, although Walter Haffkine is the only one to have left a significant mark. There has also been a trickle of truth-seekers who joined Hindu or Buddhist circles and who warrant study.

SCHOLARLY STUDIES

Bhargavam, S., 'Women Writing India: A Study of Prose Fiction by Ruth Prawer Jhabvala, Nayantara Sahgal and Shashi Deshpande' (M. Phil. thesis, University of York (U.K.), 1996).

Bhatti, Anil, 'Willy Haas and Exile in India,' in Anil Bhatti and Johannes H. Voigt, eds., *Jewish Exile in India 1933-1945* (New Delhi: Manohar, 1999): 113-26.

Bhatti, Anil and Johannes H. Voigt, eds., *Jewish Exile in India 1933-1945* (New Delhi: Manohar, 1999).

Bodhi, Bhikkhu, 'Ven. Nyanaponika Mahathera: A Vision of the Dhamma for Our Time,' *Middle Way* 71, no. 4 (February 1996): 243-58.

Chitrapu, Devi S., 'Passions and Precepts of India: A Selected Study of Ruth Prawer Jhabvala's Social Comedies' (M.A. thesis, Slippery Rock University, Pennsylvania, 1992): li + 82 pp.

Dengele, Rajendra, '*Ranangan* or Response in Marathi Literature to the Theme of Jewish Emigration,' in Anil Bhatti and Johannes H. Voigt, eds., *Jewish Exile in India 1933-1945* (New Delhi: Manohar, 1999): 172-85.

Kampchen, Martin, 'Alex Aronson: Refugee from Nazi Germany in Santiniketan,' in Anil Bhatti and Johannes H. Voigt, eds., *Jewish Exile in India 1933-1945* (New Delhi: Manohar, 1999): 127-49.

Khanna, Krishen, 'To Rudolph von Leyden: A Letterout of Season,' in Anil Bhatti and Johannes H. Voigt, eds., *Jewish Exile in India 1933-1945* (New Delhi: Manohar, 1999): 186-9.

Lotz, Rainer and Rekha Kamath, 'Interculturality: A View from Below Anita Desai's *Baumgartner's Bombay*,' in Anil Bhatti and Johannes H. Voigt, eds., *Jewish Exile in India 1933-1945* (New Delhi: Manohar, 1999): 163-71.

Oesterheld, Joachim, 'British Policy towards German-speaking Emigrants in India,' in Anil Bhatti and Johannes H. Voigt, eds., *Jewish Exile in India 1933-1945* (New Delhi: Manohar, 1999): 45-54.

Robbins, Kenneth X., 'The Camp for Polish Refugee Children at Balachadi, Nawanagar,' *Journal of Indo-Judaic Studies* (Saskatoon) 4 (2001): 95-117.

Roland, Joan G., 'Review of Bhatti and Voigt (1999),' *Jewish Studies Newsletter* 16 (1999) www.js-network@uoise.utoronto.ca

Sareen, Tilak Rai, 'Indian Responses to the Holocaust,' in Anil Bhatti and Johannes H. Voigt, eds., *Jewish Exile in India 1933-1945* (New Delhi: Manohar, 1999): 55-63.

Schindler, Agata, 'Walter Kaufmann: A Forgotten Genius,' in Anil Bhatti and Johannes H. Voigt, eds., *Jewish Exile in India 1933-1945* (New Delhi: Manohar, 1999): 87-112.

Shatrushalyasinji, H.H. the Jamsaheb of Nawanagar, 'Holocaust Refugees and the Maharaja of Jamnagar,' *Journal of Indo-Judaic Studies* 3 (2000): 137-9.

Shepherd, Ronald, *Ruth Prawer Jhabvala in India: The Jewish Connection* (Delhi: Chanakya Publications, 1994).

Siddiqi, Majid Hayat, 'Jews and Central European Nationals in Exile in Colonial India between the Two World Wars,' in Anil Bhatti and Johannes H. Voigt, eds., *Jewish Exile in India 1933-1945* (New Delhi: Manohar, 1999): 55-63.

Stier, Oren Baruch, 'Review of Anil Bhatti and Johannes Voigt, eds., *Jewish Exile in India: 1933-1945* (1999),' *Journal of Indo-Judaic Studies* (Saskatoon) 4 (2001): 127-31.

Voigt, Johannes H., 'Under the Spell of the Mahatma: Dr. Margarete Spiegel,' in Anil Bhatti and Johannes H. Voigt, eds., *Jewish Exile in India 1933-1945* (New Delhi: Manohar, 1999): 150-60.

Weil, Shalva, 'From Persecution to Freedom: Central European Jewish Refugees and their Jewish Host Communities in India,' in Anil Bhatti and Johannes H. Voigt, eds., *Jewish Exile in India 1933-1945* (New Delhi: Manohar, 1999): 64-84.

Werner, Karel, 'Venerable Nyanaponika Mahathera 1901-1994.' *Middle Way* (London) 70, no. 4 (February 1995): 267-9.

Yaakov, Yosef, 'An Overlooked Experience,' *Jerusalem Post* (10 September 1999): B12. [Review of Bhatti and Voigt, 1999.]

MEMOIRS, NOVELS, AND GENERAL ACCOUNTS

Chattopadhyaya, Harindranath, *Lotte: The Power of Love: The Life-Story of Lotte Nivelli* (Delhi: B.R. Publishing Corp., 1991).

Cohen, David Haskell, *Angels, Snakes and Ladders: Memoirs of a Jew from British India* (rev. edn., Netivot, Tonaty; London, Mr. M. Shaw, 2001 [2000]).

Dandekar, B.B., *A Nazi Among Jews* (Lawrence, KS: A.B. Literary House, 1990). [A novel reviewed by Morton I. Teicher, 'An Indian Jew in Kansas Remembers Buchenwald,' *Broward Jewish World* (3-9 January 1992): 8B.]

———, *The Jewish Amendment* (Lawrence, KS: A.B. Literary House, 1992). [A novel.]

Desai, Anita, *Baumgartner's Bombay* (New York: A.A. Knopf, 1989). [A novel.]

———, *Baumgartner's Bombay* (Boston: Houghton Mifflin, 2000).

Elijah, Samuel H., 'India Commemorates Waldemar Haffkine,' *Judaica Post: Journal of Philatelic Judaica* 10 (5721/1960): 73-4.

Fine, Arnold, 'Dr. W.M. Haffkine (1860-1930) Saved Tens of Thousands With Vaccine for Cholera And Plague,' *Jewish Press* (Brooklyn, 19 August 2003): M14.

Kakutani, Michiko, 'Review of Desai (1989),' *New York Times* (14 March 1989): C-21.

Liorard, Corrine, 'Otherness in Anita Desai's *Baumgartner's Bombay*,' in Anne Luyat and Francine Tolron, eds., *Flight from Certainty: The Dilemma of Identity and Exile* (Amsterdam and New York: Rodopo, 2001): 112-22.

Nivelli, Mickey, 'She Shattered Every Religious, Racial, and Ethnic Barrier Built Between Babies Belonging to God,' *News India-Times* (New York, 26 January 1966): 43. [About Lotte Nivelli.]

Preschel, Tovia, 'Waldermar Haffine (Mordecai Zev) on the 70th Anniversary of His Death,' *Brooklyn Jewish Press* (13 October 2000): 43; (20 October 2000): 87; (27 October 2000): 71; (3 November 2000): 45; (12 November 2000): 39; (17 November 2000): 11; (24 November 2000): 34; and (1 December 2000): 43, 76.

Shatrushalyasinji, His Highness, 'Holocaust Refugees and the Maharaja of Jamnagar,' *Journal of Indo-Judaic Studies* (Saskatoon) 3 (2000): 137-9.

Shedde, Meenakshi, 'Shalom Bombay! Hundreds of Jewish Refugees Fleeing the Nazi Terror of the War Years Settled in Mumbai and Galvanised the Cultural Life of the City,' *Sunday Times of India* (19 August 1997): 19.

Shepherd, Ronald, *Ruth Prawer Jhabvala in India: The Jewish Connection* (Delhi: Chanakya Publications, 1994).

Tokayer, Marvin, trans., 'From Japan to Palestine via Colombo with a Hasidic Journalist in 1941,' *Journal of Indo-Judaic Studies* 5 (Saskatoon) (June 2002): 69-72.

CHAPTER 7

Tribal Jews

In recent years significant numbers of Chin-kuki tribals of far north-eastern India, the Chin state of Burma and the Chittagong region of Bangladesh have embraced Judaism. Inspired by dreams and revelations, they seek study, conversion and, ultimately, emigration to Israel.

As their home regions are unsettled areas, which until recently have been strictly off limits to foreigners, knowledge of them is limited to a few academic papers by Samra (1991, 1992) and some newspaper and magazine pieces, the best of which are by Banerjie (1986) and Katz and Goldberg (1989, 1992). Benjamin's and Sawgtinlam's pamphlets (both n.d.) uniquely portray the group's self-understanding.

PRIMARY DOCUMENTS/MEMOIRS

Anonymous, *B'nei Menashe Community Mizoram Silver Jubilee 1976-2001 SOUVENIR* (Mizoram: B'nei Menashe Community, no date [2002?]).

Bene Ephraim Community of Elders, *Bene Ephraim*, unpublished manuscript (Vijayawada, Andhra Pradesh, *c*. 1996.

Benjamin, V.L., *The United Tribal Jews of the Far Northeast India* (Manipur: Beyth Sholom Prayer Hall, n.d.).

Benjamin, V.L. and Y. Stephen, *Mongoloid Israels of Manipur State* (Bualzang: Manipur Jewish Organization, 1972).

Hangshing, T. and L. Meccabi, *Brakhoth* (Manipur: Sheveth Menashe, 1994). [In Thadou Kuki.]

Quol Ha-Shafar, occasional publication edited by T. Hangshin, 5 issues as of May 1994 (Manipur: Shevet Menashe). [In Thadou Kuki.]

Sawgtinlam, *The Tuklemsom Tribe* (Kangpokpi, India: H. Scilal Press, n.d.).

Tual, Lian, Private correspondence with Katz, 1987-9.

Yacobi, Sadok, 'Brief History of the Telugu Jewish Communities of Andhra Pradesh (A.P.), India,' typescript, 1998.

Yacobi, Shmuel, *History of the Bene-Ephraim Communities of Andhra Pradesh, India* (Vijayawada: Shmuel Yacobi, n.d. [1997]).

Zaithanchhungi, *Israel-Mizo Identity* (Aizawl, Mizoram: St. Joseph's Press, 1990).

ACCOUNTS OF TRIBAL JEWS

Abdo, Geneive, 'A Torah Goes to India Where a "Lost Tribe Awaits," *Chicago Tribune Online Edition* (26 April 2004). <www.chicago tribune.com/news/printedition chi0404260125 apr26.1.754213.story?coll+chi-printnews hed>

Ahmed, Syed Zubair, 'Mizo Jews Await Return to Israel,' *The Times of India* (15 February 1994): 7.

Alpert, Carl, 'Inside Israel: Who will Storm Israel's Gates?,' *Cherry Hill (NJ) Voice* (2 February 1994): 17.

Anonymous, 'The Karens of Burma: Their Jewish Traditions,' *Missionary Herald* (Missionary Board of the Presbyterian Church of Ireland, 1 February 1887).

———, 'Lost Tribe in India Seeks Link to Jewry,' *United Israel Bulletin* 29, 3 (December 1972/Teveth 5733).

———, 'No Israeli visas for Mizo Jews,' *The Telegraph* (Calcutta, 28 February 1987).

———, 'Shinlungs Pursue Judaism in Hindu Land: Despite Difficulties, Tribe in India Claims to be Manasseh's Descendants,' *Atlanta Constitution* (9 May 1987).

———, 'India's "Mizo Jews",' *Jerusalem Post* (31 August 1989): 5.

———, 'Members of "Lost Tribe" from India will Convert and

Work in Gush Katif,' *Jerusalem Post* (7 August 1993): 24.

———, 'Most Mizos Likely to Re-Embrace Judaism in Coming Decades,' *News India-Times* (New York, 25 February 1994): 22.

———, 'Families of "Little Israel" to Emigrate,' *News India-Times* (New York, 11 March 1994): 22.

———, 'Wait for Messiah, Israel Tells "Lost Tribe" — Indian Claim Link to Ancient Menashe,' *Boston Globe* (17 August 1994).

———, '300 Million Indians Seek "Return" To Israel as Descendants of Menashe,' *Brooklyn Jewish Press* (18 August 1994): 34.

———, 'Who Is a Jew? Fearing a Floodtide, Israel may Limit Law on Immigration,' *Newark Star-Ledger* (26 August 1994): 25.

———, 'Lost Children of Israel want to Return to the Promised Land,' *Sunday Express* (4 September 1994).

———, '57 Indian Jews Migrate to Israel,' *News India-Times* (14 October 1994): 8.

———, 'Israel's "Lost Tribe" Puzzle,' *Australian Jewish News* (9 December 1994): 20.

———, 'Bnei Menashe Return Home after 2600 Years,' *Arutz-7* [electronic news] (13 February 2000).

———, 'Bnei Menashe Produce Tallitot, Kippot,' *Kulanu 8*, no. 1 (Silver Spring, MD, 2001): 1.

———, ' "Lost Tribe" Gets a New Jewish Educational Center in India,' *Arutz Sheva* (20 April 2004). IsraelNN.com

———, 'Israel's "lost tribe" in India may be Allowed to Immigrate,' *Hindustan Times* (Online, Press Trust of India, 11 August 2004).

———, 'New IDF "Olim" from India to Reunite with Their Families.' *Ma'ariv International On-line* (3 November 2004). www.maarivintl.com/com/index.cfm?fiseaction =article&articleID=11525

———, 'International Newstime: Bnei Menashe Community of India,' *Kol India* 8, no. 2 (Mumbai, December 2004): 14.

———, 'Jewish Stories for a Lost Tribe in Israel,' *Arutz-7 Israel National News* (17 December 2004). www.israelnationalnews .com/news.php3?id=73757

———, 'Rabbinate Recognizes Bnei Menashe as "Descendants of Israel",' *Arutz 7 Israel National News* (31 March 2005). http://www.israelnationalnews.com/news.php3?id=79370

———, 'Rabbi Backs India's "Lost Jews",' *BBC News* (1 April 2005). http://newsvote.bbc.co.uk/mpapps/pagetools/print/news.bbc.co. uk/2/south_asia/4400957.stm

———, 'Indians make up Largest Immigrant Group in Gaza,' *Indian Express Online* (3 August 2005). http://www.express india.com/fullstory/php?newsid=52021& headline

Arnold, Michael, 'Menashe's Children?' *Jerusalem Post International Edition* (25 April 1998): 16-17. [Reprinted: 'The Shinlung in Israel: Are They Descendants of Menashe?' *Brooklyn Jewish Press* (24 April 1998): 51, 53, 85.]

———, 'Members of India's Shinlung Tribe Continue to Trickle Quietly into Israel,' *Manhattan Jewish Sentinel* (5 June 1998): 9, 16, 17.

Avihail, Ehiahu, 'The Shinlung Are Growing!' *Kulanu* 1/2 (Summer 1994): 1.

———, 'How I Happened to "Discover" the Bnei Menasha,' in Karen Primack, ed., *Jews in Places You Never Thought Of* (New York: KTAV, 1998): 31-7.

———, 'Needed: $800 per Bnei Menashe Immigrant,' *Kulanu* (Silver Spring, Md.) 6, no. 4 (Winter 1999-2000): 5. [Letter.]

———, *Shinlung Fate: Shevet Menashe* (pamphlet, no data, *c.* 2004). [In Shinlung.]

———, 'Rabbi Backs India's "Lost Jews",' *Points East* 20/2 (Palo Alto, CA, July 2005): 4.

Avichail, Eliahu, Bruce Terris, Allenby Sela, Jack Zeller, Diane Seller, and Yaacov Levi, 'Chronology of a Successful Return,' in Karen Primack, ed., *Jews in Places You Never Thought Of* (New York: KTAV, 1998): 38-50.

Banerjie, Indranil, 'Search of the Lost Tribe,' *India Today* (15 September 1986): 72-3.

Bashi, Sari, 'Lost Jewish Tribe Wants Israeli Home,' Associated Press http://www.infobeat.com/stories/cgi/story.cgi?id=2563201810 (11 January 2000). [Reprinted as 'Indian tribe wants Israel to let them in,' *Miami Jewish Herald* (19 January 2000): 29JH.]

Benjamin, J.M., 'The Lost Tribe in Manipur,' *Ohr* (New Delhi) 24 (April 1988): 3-5.

Berindranath, D., 'Mythology of Zionist propaganda . . . Mizos are the 14th lost tribe of Israel!' *Blitz* (29 March 1980): 7.

Bernstein, Richard, 'A Quest for a People Who May No Longer Exist,' *New York Times* (18 September 2002), B6. [Review of Hillel Halkin, *Across the Sabbath River* (2002).]

Bhattacharya, Tathagata, 'The New Jerusalem – Exclusive: DNA Tests Prove that Mizo People are Descendants of a Lost Israeli Tribe,' *The Week* (12 September 2004). www.the-week.com/24sept12/currentevents.article1.htm

Bhaumik, Subir, 'Mizo "Jews" seek Israel Visas,' *BBC News World Edition* (23 December 2003).http://news.bbc.co.uk/south.asia/3228054.stm

Bollag, Raphael, 'The Ten Lost Tribes of Israel,' *Jewish City Guide of Switzerland/Jüdischer Almanach der Schweiz* 1 (1992): 23-8. [Interview with Rabbi A. Avihail.]

Bresler, Jack, 'Just Who are the Shinlung?' *Amishav USA* 1, 1 (Autumn 1993): 2-3.

———, 'Just Who are the Shinlung?' in Karen Primack, ed., *Jews in Places You Never Thought Of* (New York: KTAV, 1998): 27-30.

Chakraborty, Sanat K., 'Promised Land Beckons Jews "lost" in India,' *The Pioneer* (New Delhi, 19 July 2002).

Chowdhury, Jyoti Lal, 'The Mizos' Journey to Israel: Ascent to the Promised Land,' *Guwahati Sunday Sentinel*, 12, 29 (30 October 1994): 1.

———, 'Mizo-Jewish Root: "Return of the Native in Trouble",' *Pine Queen* (February 1995): 2-3.

Claude, Patrice, 'The Falashas of Mizoram Look in Hope to Zion,' *Manchester Guardian Weekly* (19 April 1987): 12.

Devi, Sharmila, 'Test of "Jewishness" faces Indians Longing for Israel,' *Los Angeles Times* (15 August 2004): 2.

Duker, Jonina, 'A New Ritual for Passover: Honoring the Return of a Lost Tribe,' in Karen Primack, ed., *Jews in Places You Never Thought Of* (New York: KTAV, 1998): 51-2.

Elliman, Wendy, 'Menashe's Children Come Home,' *Hadassah Magazine* (New York), 81, no. 2 (October 1999): 22-6. [Photographs by Mirian Sushman.]

Epstein, Lawrence J., 'In Search of the Ten Lost Tribes,' *Jewish Action* (no data available): 54-9.

Fine, Arnold, 'The Lost Tribes: The Search for the Remnants of Israel,' *Jewish Press* (Brooklyn) (8 October 2004): M8; Part II, (15 October 2004): M8.

Fleischmann, Kurt, 'Are They the Tribe of Menashe?' *London Scribe* 63 (March 1995).

Foster, Peter, 'India's Lost Tribe Recognized as Jews after 2,700 Years,' *News.telegraph* (UK, 17 September 2005).

Francisco, Jason L., 'Meet the Telegu Jews of India,' *Kulanu* 2, 3 (1995): 1, 7-8.

———, ' "Discovering" the Telegu Jews of India,' in Karen Primack, ed., *Jews in Places You Never Thought Of* (New York: KTAV, 1998): 253-62.

Franks, Suzanne, 'The Lost Tribe of Manipur,' *The Jewish Quarterly* (London) 3 (1987): 32-4.

———, 'Jews of Manipur: The Lost Tribe,' *India Worldwide* 2, 10 (May 1989): 52-5.

Freund, Michael, '4 Rabbis Visit Bnei Menashe in India,' *Kulanu* 9, no. 1 (Silver Spring MD, Spring 2992): 1, 16-17.

———, 'Long-lost Jews,' *Jerusalem Post Magazine* (27 March 2002).

———, 'Bring the Bnei Menashe Home to Israel,' *Jerusalem Post* (25 July 2002). [Reprinted in *Kulanu* 8, no. 2 (Silver Spring MD, Summer 2002): 6, and again in *Kulanu* 12, no. 1 (Spring 2005): 2.

———, 'Manasseh's Children,' in Karen Primack, ed., *Under One Canopy: Readings in Jewish Diversity* (Silver Spring MD, Kulanu, 2003): 117-21.

———, 'Finding a lost tribe of Israel,' *WorldnetDaily* (5 July 2005). http://www.worldnetdaily.com/news/asp?ARTI CLE_ ID=45118

———, 'Building Mikvahs in India for Bnei Menashe,' *Arutz Sheva Israel National News* (14 Tammus 5765/ 21 July 2005). http:// www.israelnational.news.com/news.php3?id=86248

Friedman, Ina, 'By the Rivers of Babylon,' *Jerusalem Report* (19 May 2003): 14-19.

Gabow, Leo, 'The Jews of Manipur,' *Points East* 1, 3 (September 1986): 3.

Ghosal, Vivek, 'Do the Mizos hail from Israel?' *Sunday Observer* (9-15 November 1997): 2.

Ghosh, S., 'Tribal Jews set up Campaign for Recognition,' *The Telegraph* (Calcutta, 10 March 1988): 7.

Golan, Yehida, 'Milyon Ahrnu b'Hodu,' *Ma'ariv* (28 August 1991): 3. [In Hebrew.]

Gordon, Baruch, '200 Bnei Menashe in India Convert to Judaism,' *Arutz Sheva* (Jerusalem, 21 September 2005).

Haberman, Clyde, ' "Lost Tribe" Has Israelis Pondering Law of Return,' *New York Times* (6 October 1994): A3.

Halkin, Hillel, 'Wandering Jews: And Their Genes,' *Commentary* 110/2 (New York, September 2000): 54-61.

———, 'Across the Sabbath River,' *Jerusalem Post Magazine* (9 August 2002): 6-10.

———, *Across the Sabbath River: In Search of a Lost Tribe of Israel* (Boston and New York: Houghton Mifflin Company, 2002).

Hookip, Benyamin, 'Bnei Menashe in India Need Books,' *Kulanu* (Silver Spring, Md.) 6, no. 4 (Winter 1999-2000): 4. [Letter.]

Husain, Wasbir, 'Migrating to the Promised Land,' *The Telegraph* (Calcutta, 24 November 1991): 11.

———, 'Exodus to Promised Land,' *India Abroad* (10 January 1992): 18. [Filed with Chhaya 1992.]

Hussain, Syed Zarir, 'India: The Lost Jews of Mizoram,' *Religioscope* (16 December 2003). http://religioscope.info/article_ 250.shtml

Jain, Sonu, 'An Indo-Israel Story, from North-East to West Bank,' *Indian Express* (Bombay, 21 September 2003): 1.

Karmakar, Rahul, 'Holy Smoke in NE over Promise Land,' *Hindustan Times* (7 May 2005). www.hindustantimes.com/onlineCDA/PFVersion.jsp?article=http:/ /10.81.141.122/news/5922_1352869.00150021999999999.htm

Katz, Nathan and Ellen S. Goldberg, 'The Mysterious Chin-kuki Tribal Jews of the Indo-Burmese Border Regions,' *Journal of the American Association of Rabbis* 5, 1 (1989): 11-19.

———, 'Dreams and Visions Beckon Remote Indo-Burmese Tribals to Judaism,' *Journal of the Society of Rabbis in Academia* 2, 2 (1992): 47-57.

Keinon, Herb, 'Finding Room for All the Lost Tribes,' *Jerusalem Post International Edition* (17 September 1994): 8A.

———, ' "Lost Tribes" Claim Connection to Israel,' *Philadelphia Jewish Exponent* 9 (16 September 1994): 27.

Klein, Aaron, ' "Lost Tribe" of Israel Faces Summer Evac,' *WorldNetDaily* (5 July 2005). http://www.worldnetdailu.com/news/asp?ARTICLE_ID=45124. [Also in *Jewish Press* (Brooklyn, 15 July 2005): 12.]

———, 'Rabbis Convert "Lost Tribe" of Israel,' *WorldNetDaily* (26 September 2005).

Klein Halevi, Yossi, 'Return of the Lost Tribes,' *Jerusalem Report* (9 September 1993): 12-17.

———, 'The Unwanted Immigrants,' *Points East* 10, 1 (March 1995): 8-9. [Reprint from *Jerusalem Report* (17 November 1994).]

———, 'Israel Cancels Visas for Would-Be Indian Converts,' *Points East* 10, 1 (March 1995): 9.

Krausz, Tibor, 'Zion on the Myanmar Border,' *Jerusalem Reports* (17 November 2003): L 106-11.

Lavender, Abraham D., 'Review of Primack, ed., *Jews in Places You Never Thought Of* (1998),' *Journal of Indo-Judaic Studies* (Saskatoon) 2 (1999): 146-8.

Lewin, Avrohom Shmuel, 'Israeli Leftists Call for Amending the

Law of Return,' *Brooklyn Jewish Press* (26 August-1 September 1994).

Lobatzky, Galit, 'My Dream was to Join the Israeli Army,' *B'Machaney* (Israel Defense Forces Newspaper, 23 July 2004). [In Hebrew.]

Lobo, Melvyn, 'Kuki, Lost Jewish Tribe, Finds Its Roots,' *News India-Times* (29 October 1993): 21.

Maimon, Isaac, 'The Ten Lost Tribes,' *Lashon* (Seattle, September-October 1998): 6.

Malcioln, José V., 'The Tribal Jews of Northeast India,' *The African Origin of Modern Judaism: From Hebrews to Jews* (Trenton NJ: Africa World Press, 1996): 435-40.

Mandel, Eli, 'Bring Us Home,' *Jewish Homemaker* (Adar II 5755/ February 1995): 16-21.

Margolis, David, 'Finding the Lost Tribes,' *The Reporter* 48, 4 (1998): 14-18.

Marshall, Jon, 'Havdallah in Uganda: Jewish Life has Taken Root in Unexpected Places, from the Forests of India to the Island of Singapore to a Village in Uganda,' *Reform Judaism* (Spring 1999): 64-8.

Morris, Nomi, 'The Jews of Asia: Canadians Urge Israel to Aid a "Lost Tribe",' *Macleans* (10 August 1998): 27-8.

Mukerji, Debashish, 'On Mizo Hills, They Dream of Zion: Back to Menassiah,' *This Week* (16 July 1989).

Musleah, Rahel, 'Menashe's Children? One Man's Search for the Ten Lost Tribes,' *Manhattan Jewish Sentinel* (5 June 1998): 6, 9.

Myre, Greg, ' "Lost Tribe" Finds Itself on Front Lines of Mideast Conflict,' *New York Times* (22 December 2003).

Naresh, N., 'To Reach the Promised Land,' *Deccan Chronicle* (Vijayawada, 12 September 2004).

Nevins, Michael and Ted Nevins, 'The Born-Again Jews of Mizoram and Manipur,' unpublished manuscript, 1994.

Orr, David, 'Squeezed between Burma and Bangladesh, "descendants" of the Lost Tribes of Israel Convert to Judaism,' *News Telegraph* (19 September 2005).

Pandey, Geeta, 'India's "lost Jews" Wait in Hope,' *BBC News World Edition* (18 August 2004). http://news.bbc.co.uk/2/hi/south.asia/3575716.stm

Panitz, Beth, 'Long-Lost Jews: In a Remote Corner of India, Judaism Thrives,' *Babaganewz* (Israel, Adar I, 5765/April, 2005): 14-16.

Parfitt, Tudor, 'The Land of Hard Bondage: The Lost Tribes in India,' *Journal of Indo-Judaic Studies* (Saskatoon) 5 (June 2002): 55-68.

———, 'The Land of Hard Bondage' and 'The Burmese Frontier: The Land of Strangers,' in *The Lost Tribes of Israel: The History of a Myth* (London: Weidenfeld & Nicolson, 2002): 117-31, 132-44.

———, 'Tribal Jews.' Paper read at 'A View from the Margin: The State of the Art of Indo-Judaic Studies,' Oxford Centre for Hebrew and Jewish Studies, U.K., 2-6 July 2002.

———, 'In Search of the Lost Tribes,' *World Jewish Digest* 1, 9 (Skokie IL, May 2004): 24-5, 45-6.

Rabin, Eitan, 'Their Homes May be far Away: But Their Hearts Are in Israel,' *Ma'ariv Online* (9 May 2005).

Rabinowitz, Gavin, 'Israeli "Lost Tribes" Living in W. Bank,' *Yahoo! News/Associated Press* (24 December 2003).

———, ' "Lost Tribe of Israel" Living in West Bank Settlements,' *World Jewish Digest* 1, 9 (Skokie IL, May 2004): 18.

Radpszkpwocz, Abogail, 'Team Probes Lost Tribe in India,' *Jerusalem Post Online Edition* (11 August 2004). www.jpost.com/servlet/Satellite?/pagename=Jpost/JPArticle/Printer&cid=1092193811331&p=1008596975996

Rei, Gideon, 'Is the Door Closing on Manipur Jews?' *India Worldwide* 2, 11 (June 1989): 5.

Riskin, Shlomo, 'My Visit to the Bnei Menashe Tribe in India,' *Jewish Press* (Brooklyn, 7 February 2003): 36. [Reprinted in *Points East* (Silver Spring, Md.) 18, 1 (March 2003): 16.]

———, 'Weekly Portion: On the Wings of our Children,' *Jerusalem Post International Edition* (27 February 2004): 31.

Rosenbluth, Susan, 'Israeli Rabbinate Recognizes Northeast Indian Bnei Menashe as "Descendants of Israel",' *National Jewish Post and Opinion* (2005), no data available.

Ruby, Walter, 'Manipuri Jews Wait for Word,' *Jerusalem Post* (13 September 1985).

Samra, Myer, 'The Tribe of Manasseh: "Judaism" in the Hills of Manipur and Mizoram,' *Man in India* 71, 1 (1991): 183-202.

———, 'Judaism in Manipur and Mizoram: By-Product of Christian Mission,' in J.V. Hluna, et al., eds., *Seminar Papers: Studies on the Minority Nationalities of Northeast India—The Mizos* (Aizawl: Directorate of Higher and Technical Education, Government of Mizoram, 1992): 63-7.

———, 'The Bene Menasseh: Tribal Jews of North East India,' *Encyclopedia Judaica Yearbook*, 1992.

———, 'Judaism in Manipur and Mizoram: By-Product of Christian Mission,' *Australian Journal of Jewish Studies* 6, 1 (1992): 7-22.

———, 'Review of Isenberg (1988),' *Israel Social Science Research* 8, 2 (1993): 102-5.

———, 'India's Despised Lovers of Zion,' *Jerusalem Post International Edition* (10 September 1994): 6.

———, 'True Converts of Honor,' *Jerusalem Post* (16 October 1994).

———, 'Defending the Bnei Menasheh,' *Jerusalem Report* (29 December 1994): 3. [Letter-to-the-editor.]

———, 'In Search of the Lost Tribes: For Rabbi Eliyahu Avihail, the Search for the World's "Lost" Jews is his Life's Work,' *New Moon: Australia's Jewish Lifestyle Magazine* (September-October 1995): 24-5.

———, 'Struggling to be Jewish,' *Generation: A Journal of Australian Jewish Life, Thought and Community* 5, 2 (September 1995).

———, 'Buallawn Israel: The Emergence of a Judaising Movement in Mizoram, Northeast India,' in L. Olson, ed., *Religious Change, Conversion and Culure* 12 (Sydney, 1996): 105-31.

———, 'Opinion: Bring in the Bene Menashe,' *Kulanu* (Silver Spring, MD) 8, no. 4 (2001-02): 5.

Schwartz, Bryan, 'From the Road in Manipur,' *Kulanu* 7 (Silver Spring, MD, Winter 2000-01): 1, 14.

Shahan, Avigdor, *Toward the Sambatyon River: A Journey in the Footsteps of the Ten Tribes* (Tel Aviv: Hakibutz Hameuchad, 2003): [In Hebrew.]

Shanks, Hershel, 'Is the Remnant of a Tribe of Manasseh Living in Northeast India?' Forum review of Hillel Halkin, *Across the Sabbath River: In Search of a Lost Tribe of Israel* (New York: Houghton Mifflin, 2002). [Includes: Rivka Gonen, 'The Cultural View' and Ronald Hendel, 'The Linguistic View,' *Biblical Archaeology Review* (September/October 2003): 78-81.]

Shanson, Lindsay, ' "Lost tribe" found in Burma,' *London Jewish Chronicle* (29 August 1986): 17.

———, ' "Lost Tribe" Found in Burma,' *Points East* 1, 3 (September 1986): 8.

———, 'Twilight in Burma,' no publication data.

Sharma, Devinder, 'More of India's Mizo Jews Planning Immigration,' *Jerusalem Post* (21 February 1994): 12.

Sharrow, Barnard G., 'Isolated Jewish Community at Manipur Seeks Contacts with World Jewry; Claim Descent from "Lost" Menasseh Tribe,' *United Israel Bulletin* 41, 3 (December 1984/ Kislev 5745): 4.

Steinberg, Jessica, ' "Lost Tribe" from India Adjusts to Life After Aliyah,' *Jewish Exponent* (Philadelphia, 26 December 2002).

Stephens, Bert, 'Bookshelf: Journey to the East,' *Jerusalem Post* (9 August 2002): 4. [Review of Hillel Halkin, *Across the Sabbath River* (2002).]

———, 'His own Lost Tribe,' *Jerusalem Post Magazine* (9 August 2002): 12. [Interview with Hillel Halkin.]

Stutz, Eli, 'Search for "Lost" Jews Leads to Spain, Brazil and India,' *Canadian Jewish News* (9 June 2005). http://www.cjnews.com/viewarticle.asp?id=6576

Subhani, Syed Zarir, 'Mizo Jews: To Their Promised Land,' *Sun* 17, 27 (29 January-4 February 1994): 16.

Terris, Bruce, 'My Visit with the Shinlung Immigrants,' *Amishav USA* 1, 1 (Autumn 1993): 1-2.

———, 'Bnei Menashe Update,' *Kulanu* 61 (Spring 1999): 14.

Tommer, Yohanathan, 'Return of a Lost Tribe,' *The Hindu* (23 March 1994).

Tsur, Batsheva, 'Uri Gordon: Time to Change Law of Return,' *Jerusalem Post International Edition* (27 August 1994): 2.

Urden, Jonathan, 'The Long Journey Home,' *Jewish Action* 64, no. 2 (New York, Winter 2003): 50-3.

Wagner, Mathew, 'Bnei Menashe find Home Over Green Line: Plan in Full Swing for Mass Conversion of 6,000-7,000 Members of Tribe in India,' *Jerusalem Post* (6 April 2005): 1, 9.

———, 'Bnei Menashe Conversions Halted,' *Jerusalem Post* (9 November 2005).

Weil, Shalva, 'Beyond The Sambatyon: The Myth of the Ten Lost Tribes,' *Ariel* 85-86 (1991): 25-31.

———, 'Double Conversion among the "Children of Menasseh",' in Ely Ben-Gal, ed., *The People of the Menorah* (Tel Aviv: Maccabi World Union, 1995): 84-102.

———, 'Dual Conversion among the Shinlung of North-East India,' *Tribes and Tribals* 1/1 (2003): 43-57.

———, 'Lost Israelites from the Indo-Burmese Borderlands: Re-Traditionalisation and Conversion Among the Shinlung or Bene Menasseh,' *The Anthropologist* 6, 3 (2004): 219-33.

Weintraub, Richard M., 'Group in India Yearns to Be Jewish,' *Washington Post* (16 March 1987).

———, 'Group in India Yearns to Be Jewish,' *Points East* 3, 1 (February 1988): 5.

Weisman, Steven R., 'In India, Jewish Sect Claims Ties to Long-Lost Israeli Tribe,' *International Herald Tribune* (25 February 1987)

———, 'Mizo Jews Want to Return "Home",' *The Times of India* (Bombay, 6 March 1987).

Weiss, Steven I., 'Right-wing Initiative Targets "Lost Jews",' *Forward* (New York, 28 May 2004): 5.

Zeller, Jack, 'A Truly Unique Seminary,' *Kulanu* (Silver Spring, Md.) 3, no. 3 (Autumn 1996): 1, 7.

———, 'Bnei Menashe Synagogue,' *Kulanu* (Silver Spring, Md.) 6, no. 4 (Winter 1999-2000): 9.

VIDEOTAPE

Be-'ikvot ha-shevatim ha-avudim Mizorem (Yerushalayim: Tel'ad, 1998).